SOUTH-WESTERN
LAW FOR BUSINESS AND PERSONAL USE

LESSON PLANS

ADAMSON-MIETUS

15TH EDITION

VISIT US ON THE INTERNET
www.swep.com

South-Western Educational Publishing

an International Thomson Publishing company I(T)P®

WWW: http://www.thomson.com

Cincinnati • Albany, NY • Belmont, CA • Bonn • Boston • Detroit • Johannesburg • London • Madrid
Melbourne • Mexico City • New York • Paris • Singapore • Tokyo • Toronto • Washington

I(T)P®

International Thomson Publishing

South-Western Educational Publishing is a division of Thomson International Publishing Inc. The ITP logo is a registered trademark used herein under license by South-Western Educational Publishing.

ISBN: 0-538-68360-0

1 2 3 4 5 6 7 8 9 0 WE 03 02 01 00 99

PRINTED IN THE UNITED STATES OF AMERICA

CONDENSED TABLE OF CONTENTS

Chapter   **Page**

EXPANDED TABLE OF CONTENTS

Lesson	Page

Lesson	Page

Lesson	Page

Lesson	Page

Law for Business and Personal Use

Teacher: _____

Week of: _____

M   T   W   Th   F

Unit 1   Law, Justice, and You(Chapters 1-6)
pp. 2-95
Introduction
- In Practice Profile: Barbara Cicognani, Prison Nurse (p. 3)

Chapter 1   Our Laws
pp. 4-17
Introduction
- Hot Debate (p. 4)

Chapter 1 Teaching Resources
LAW LEARNING PACKAGE
- Unit 1 Resource Book, pp. 5-14
- Transparencies 1, 4
- Student Activities and Study Guide, pp. 1-6
- Lessons 1-1 and 1-2 Spanish Resources
- Interactive Business Law Study Guide Chapter 1
- WESTEST Chapter 1

Law for Business and Personal Use

Teacher: _____
Week of: _____

      M   T   W   Th   F

Lesson 1-1   Our Laws and Legal System
Pages 5-8

Goals
- Explain the stages in the evolution of law
- Describe the differences between common law and positive law
- Describe the difference between law courts and equity courts

Teaching Resources
LAW LEARNING PACKAGE
- Student Activities and Study Guide, pp. 1-2
- Transparencies 1, 4
- Unit 1 Resource Book, pp. 5-8
- Lesson 1-1 Spanish Resources

Focus
- Review students' ideas of what law is.
- List four stages in the growth of law.

Teach
- What Is Law? (p. 5)
- What Is the Origin of Our Legal System? (pp. 6-8)
- What's Your Verdict? (pp. 5, 6)
- Cultural Diversity in Law, *Louisiana* (p. 6)
- FYI (p. 8)
- Curriculum Connection, *History* (TE, p. 6)
- Think Critically Through Visuals (TE, p. 7)

Apply
- Think About Legal Concepts 1-5 (p. 8)
- Think Critically About Evidence 6-9 (p. 8)

Assess
- Lesson 1-1 Quiz (Unit 1 Resource Book, p. 5)
- Reteach
  Invite a local judge to speak to the class about equity in the law.
- Enrich
  Have students create a mural of the four stages in the growth of the law.

Close
- Review questions in *What's Your Verdict?* on pages 5 and 6.

Law for Business and Personal Use

Teacher: _____

Week of: _____

M   T   W   Th   F

Lesson 1-2   Types of Laws
Pages 9-13

Goals
- Explain how constitutional, statutory, case, and administrative laws are created
- Explain how to resolve conflicts between constitutional, statutory, case, and administrative laws
- Describe the differences between criminal and civil, substantive and procedural, and business and other forms of law

Teaching Resources
LAW LEARNING PACKAGE
- Student Activities and Study Guide, pp. 3-6
- Transparency 1
- Unit 1 Resource Book, pp. 9-12
- Lesson 1-2 Spanish Resources

Focus
- Discuss school and/or family laws or rules
- Discuss what changes students would like to make in these laws or rules and what effect such changes would have

Teach
- What Are the Sources of Our Laws? (pp. 9-10)
- What Happens When Laws Conflict? (pp. 10-11)
- What Are the Main Types of Laws? (pp. 11-12)
- What's Your Verdict? (pp. 9, 10, 11)
- In This Case (p. 10)
- Law in the Media (p. 12)
- Curriculum Connection, *Communication* (TE, pp. 10, 12)
- Think Critically Through Visuals (TE, p. 11)

Apply
- Think About Legal Concepts 1-9 (p. 13)
- Think Critically About Evidence 10-14 (p. 13)

Assess
- Lesson 1-2 Quiz (Unit 1 Resource Book, p. 9)
- Reteach
  Have students create a chart that shows the differences between criminal and civil law.
- Enrich
  Have students write an essay that shows that they understand the meaning of procedural and substantive law.

Close
- Read and discuss *Prevent Legal Difficulties* on page 13.
- Discuss how knowledge of business law will help students both as consumers and in the world of work.

Law for Business and Personal Use

Teacher: _____

Week of: _____

M   T   W   Th   F

Chapter 1 in Review
Pages 14-17

Teaching Resources
LAW LEARNING PACKAGE
- Chapter 1 Test (Unit 1 Resource Book, pp. 13-14)
- Interactive Business Law Study Guide Chapter 1
- WESTEST Chapter 1

Review
- Concepts in Brief 1-9 (p. 14)
- Your Legal Vocabulary 1-14 (p.14)
- Review Legal Concepts 15-20 (p. 15)
- Write About Legal Concepts 21-23 (p. 15)
- Think Critically About Evidence 24-28 (p. 15)
- Analyze Real Cases 29-33 (p. 16)

Apply
- Case for Legal Thinking (p. 17)
  - Practice Judging 1-3

Assess
- WESTEST Chapter 1
- Chapter 1 Test (Unit 1 Resource Book, pp. 13-14)

Law for Business and Personal Use

Teacher: _____
Week of: _____
　　　　　M　　　T　　　W　　　Th　　　F

Chapter 2 　　 Ethics in Our Law
pp. 18-33

Introduction
* Hot Debate (p. 18)

Chapter 2 Teaching Resources
LAW LEARNING PACKAGE
* Unit 1 Resource Book, pp. 19-32
* Transparencies 1, 2
* Student Activities and Study Guide, pp. 7-12
* Lessons 2-1, 2-2, and 2-3 Spanish Resources
* Interactive Business Law Study Guide Chapter 2
* WESTEST Chapter 2

Law for Business and Personal Use

Teacher: _____
Week of: _____
M   T   W   Th   F

Lesson 2-1   What Is Ethics?
Pages 19-21

Goals
- Define ethics
- Describe each element of the definition
- Define business ethics

Teaching Resources
LAW LEARNING PACKAGE
- Student Activities and Study Guide, pp. 7-8
- Transparencies 1, 2
- Unit 1 Resource Book, pp. 19-22
- Lesson 2-1 Spanish Resources

Focus
- Write "What does <u>ethics</u> mean?" on the board.
- Pose the situation described on TE page 19 and ask who is displaying more ethical behavior.

Teach
- Ethics Defined (pp. 19-21)
- What's Your Verdict? (p. 19)
- Cultural Diversity in Law, *International* (p. 19)
- In This Case (p. 20)

Apply
- Think About Legal Concepts 1-5 (p. 21)
- Think Critically About Evidence 6-11 (p. 21)

Assess
- Lesson 2-1 Quiz (Unit 1 Resource Book, (p. 19)
- Reteach
  Have small groups of students identify a decision recently made within the school community and discuss its ethical reasoning.
- Enrich
  Have students identify newspaper stories about something a local business has done. Have students take notes on the article and explain why the business is or is not making ethical decisions.

Close
- Review questions in *What's Your Verdict?* on page 19.

Law for Business and Personal Use

Teacher: _____
Week of: _____

M   T   W   Th   F

Lesson 2-2   Reasoning About Right and Wrong
Pages 22-24

Goals
- Reason based on consequences
- Reason using ethical rules

Teaching Resources
LAW LEARNING PACKAGE
- Student Activities and Study Guide, pp. 9-10
- Transparencies 1, 2
- Unit 1 Resource Book, pp. 23-26
- Lesson 2-2 Spanish Resources

Focus
- Write "What are consequences?" on the board.
- Guide students to see that all actions have consequences. Ask "If the end result is good, does this justify the means?"

Teach
- Basic Forms of Ethical Reasoning (pp. 22-24)
- What's Your Verdict? (p. 22)
- In This Case (p. 23)
- Think Critically Through Visuals (TE, pp. 22, 23)
- Cultural Diversity in Law (TE, p. 23)

Apply
- Think About Legal Concepts 1-6 (p. 24)
- Think Critically About Evidence 7-12 (p. 24)

Assess
- Lesson 2-2 Quiz (Unit 1 Resource Book, p. 23)
- Reteach
  Have students work in pairs to outline the lesson..
- Enrich
  Have students work in small groups to prepare a situation in which ethical reasoning can be used.

Close
- Review questions in *What's Your Verdict?* on page 22.

Law for Business and Personal Use

Teacher: _____
Week of: _____
M   T   W   Th   F

Lesson 2-3   How Is Ethics Expressed in Our Laws?
Pages 25-29

Goals
- Explain how our laws reflect ethics based on consequences and ethics based on reasoning
- Discuss why we are obligated to obey laws

Teaching Resources
LAW LEARNING PACKAGE
- Student Activities and Study Guide, pp. 11-12
- Transparencies 1, 2
- Unit 1 Resource Book, pp. 27-30
- Lesson 2-3 Spanish Resources

Focus
- Write "What is majority rule?" on the board
- Ask students why it is important to have majority rule in a community. Ask when might the majority rule be the wrong choice.

Teach
- Our Laws Reflect Ethics Based on Consequences (p. 25)
- Our Laws Reflect Rule-Based Ethics (pp. 25-26)
- Other Ethical Goals Reflected in Our Laws (p. 27)
- Why Are We Obligated to Obey Laws? (pp. 27-28)
- Are We Ever Justified in Violating the Law? (pp. 28-29)
- What's Your Verdict? (pp. 25, 27, 28)
- Law and the Internet (p. 26)
- Curriculum Connection, *Language Arts* (TE, pp. 27, 28)
- Think Critically Through Visuals (TE, p. 26)

Apply
- Think About Legal Concepts 1-6 (p. 29)
- Think Critically About Evidence 7-11 (p. 29)

Assess
- Lesson 2-3 Quiz (Unit 1 Resource Book, p. 27)
- Reteach
  Invite leaders from different religions to form a panel to discuss ethics and ethical conduct.
- Enrich
  Have students study the impeachment of President Clinton and prepare a report on the ethical conduct of the President, Congress, and the special prosecutor.

Close
- Read and discuss *Prevent Legal Difficulties* on page 29.

Law for Business and Personal Use   Teacher: _____
                                                          Week of: _____
                                                                    M   T   W   Th   F

Chapter 2 in Review
Pages 30-33

Teaching Resources
LAW LEARNING PACKAGE
- Chapter 2 Test (Unit 1 Resource Book, pp. 31-32)
- Interactive Business Law Study Guide Chapter 2
- WESTEST Chapter 2

Review
- Concepts in Brief 1-11 (p. 30)
- Your Legal Vocabulary 1-12 (p. 30)
- Review Legal Concepts 13-16 (p. 31)
- Write About Legal Concepts 17-21 (p. 31)
- Think Critically About Evidence 22-25 (p. 31)
- Analyze Real Cases 26-31 (p. 32)

Apply
- Case for Legal Thinking (p. 33)
  - Practice Judging 1-2

Assess
- WESTEST Chapter 2
- Chapter 2 Test (Unit 1 Resource Book, pp. 31-32)

Law for Business and Personal Use

Teacher: _____

Week of: _____

| M | T | W | Th | F |

Chapter 3   **Constitutional Rights**
pp. 34-51

Introduction
- Hot Debate (p. 34)

Chapter 3 Teaching Resources

LAW LEARNING PACKAGE
- Unit 1 Resource Book, pp. 38-53
- Transparencies 1, 2, 5, 6
- Student Activities and Study Guide, pp. 13-18
- Lessons 3-1, 3-2, and 3-3 Spanish Resources
- Interactive Business Law Study Guide Chapter 3
- WESTEST Chapter 3

Law for Business and Personal Use

Teacher: _____

Week of: _____

M   T   W   Th   F

Lesson 3-1   Foundations of Our Constitution
Pages 35-38

Goals
- Name the documents written in the course of our nation's founding
- Explain the relationship between the Declaration of Independence and the Constitution

Teaching Resources

LAW LEARNING PACKAGE
- Student Activities and Study Guide, pp. 13-14
- Transparency 1
- Unit 1 Resource Book, pp. 38-42
- Lesson 3-1 Spanish Resources

Focus
- Write "What are our nation's framing documents?"
- Briefly discuss each of the four framing documents.

Teach
- Our Nation's Framing Documents (pp. 35-37)
- What's Your Verdict? (p. 35)
- Cultural Diversity in Law, *England* (p. 36)
- FYI (p. 36)
- Think Critically Through Visuals (TE, p. 37)

Apply
- Think About Legal Concepts 1-9 (p. 38)
- Think Critically About Evidence 10-15 (p. 38)

Assess
- Lesson 3-1 Quiz (Unit 1 Resource Book, p. 38)
- Reteach
  Have students create a poster that celebrates the founders of this country. Have each student write a short paragraph about what makes this country great. Add these to the poster.
- Enrich
  Show the video 1776 to the class. Have students break into 13 small groups. Each group is to research a representative of one of the original 13 colonies and his position on the issues of the Declaration of Independence.

Close
- Review questions in *What's Your Verdict*? on page 35.

Law for Business and Personal Use   Teacher: _____
                                           Week of: _____
                                                    M   T   W   Th   F

Lesson 3-2   Amendments to the Constitution
Pages 39-43

Goals
- Discuss how the Constitution has been a shield against violations of basic human rights
- Identify the basic human rights protected by the Bill of Rights and subsequent amendments

Teaching Resources
LAW LEARNING PACKAGE
- Student Activities and Study Guide, pp. 15-16
- Transparencies 1, 2, 5
- Unit 1 Resource Book, pp. 43-46
- Lesson 3-2 Spanish Resources

Focus
- Write "What are the 10 amendments in the Bill of Rights?" on the board.
- Discuss how the Bill of Rights does or does not affect students' lives.

Teach
- Amendments and Rights: The Bill of Rights (pp. 39-41)
- More Constitutional Amendments (pp. 41-42)
- What's Your Verdict? (pp. 39, 41)
- Law and the Internet (p. 40)
- FYI (p. 40)
- Cultural Diversity in Law, *Wyoming* (p. 42)
- A Questions of Ethics (p. 42)
- Curriculum Connection, *Communications* (TE, p. 39)
- Curriculum Connection, *History* (TE, p. 41)
- Think Critically Through Visuals (TE, p. 42)

Apply
- Think About Legal Concepts 1-8 (p. 43)
- Think Critically About Evidence 9-14 (p. 43)

Assess
- Lesson 3-2 Quiz (Unit 1 Resource Book, p. 43)
- Reteach
  Have students write a short essay on how different life in this country would be if the Thirteenth, Fourteenth, Fifteenth, Nineteenth, and Twenty-Sixth amendments had not been added to the Constitution.
- Enrich
  Have students work in ten groups, each group taking one amendment from the Bill of Rights. Have groups create posters.

Close
- As a class, write a Bill of Rights for conduct for the class members. Post the Class Bill of Rights.

Law for Business and Personal Use

Teacher: _____

Week of: _____

M   T   W   Th   F

Lesson 3-3   Division and Balance of Powers
Pages 44-47

Goals
- Discuss how the Constitution created a system of checks and balances
- Explain how the power to govern is divided between the federal and state governments

Teaching Resources
LAW LEARNING PACKAGE
- Student Activities and Study Guide, pp. 17-18
- Transparencies 1, 6
- Unit 1 Resource Book, pp. 47-50
- Lesson 3-3 Spanish Resources

Focus
- Write "What are checks and balances?" on the board.
- Ask students why checks and balances are necessary.

Teach
- Our System of Checks and Balances (pp. 44-45)
- Does the Federal Government Have Total Governing Power? (pp. 45-46)
- What's Your Verdict? (pp. 44, 45)
- Cultural Diversity in Law, *Hungary* (p. 46)
- FYI (p. 46)
- Curriculum Connection, *History* (TE, p. 44)
- Think Critically Through Visuals (TE, p. 45)

Apply
- Think About Legal Concepts 1-8 (p. 47)
- Think Critically About Evidence 9-11 (p. 47)

Assess
- Lesson 3-3 Quiz (Unit 1 Resource Book, p. 47)
- Reteach
  Have students create a chart of the three branches of government.
- Enrich
  Have students research another democratic country to find out how the powers of their government are checked and balanced.

Close
- Read and discuss *Prevent Legal Difficulties* on page 47.
- Divide the class into two groups. Assign each group different pages from the text. Have each group write a list of questions from their text pages. Then have one group quiz the other group.

Law for Business and Personal Use

Teacher: _____
Week of: _____

| M | T | W | Th | F |

Chapter 3 in Review
Pages 48-51

Teaching Resources
LAW LEARNING PACKAGE
- Chapter 3 Test (Unit 1 Resource Book, pp. 51-53)
- Interactive Business Law Study Guide Chapter 3
- WESTEST Chapter 3

Review
- Concepts in Brief 1-10 (p. 48)
- Your Legal Vocabulary 1-11 (p.48)
- Review Legal Concepts 12-15 (p. 49)
- Write About Legal Concepts 16-19 (p. 49)
- Think Critically About Evidence 20-21 (p. 49)
- Analyze Real Cases 22-25 (p. 50)

Apply
- Case for Legal Thinking (p. 51)
  - Practice Judging 1-3

Assess
- WESTEST Chapter 3
- Chapter 3 Test (Unit 1 Resource Book, pp. 51-53)

Law for Business and Personal Use

Chapter 4   The Court System
pp. 52-65

Introduction

• Hot Debate (p. 52)

Chapter 4 Teaching Resources

LAW LEARNING PACKAGE

• Unit 1 Resource Book, pp. 59-73
• Transparencies 1, 2, 7, 8
• Student Activities and Study Guide, pp. 19-24
• Lessons 4-1, 4-2, and 4-3 Spanish Resources
• Interactive Business Law Study Guide Chapter 4
• WESTEST Chapter 4

Law for Business and Personal Use

Teacher: _____

Week of: _____

| M | T | W | Th | F |

Lesson 4-1   Dispute Resolution and the Courts
Pages 53-54

Goals
- Explain how disputes can be settled without resort to the courts
- Name the different levels of courts and describe their powers

Teaching Resources

LAW LEARNING PACKAGE
- Student Activities and Study Guide, pp. 19-20
- Transparencies 1, 7
- Unit 1 Resource Book, pp. 59-62
- Lesson 4-1 Spanish Resources

Focus
- Write "What are the two levels of our nation's courts?" on the board.
- Have students write the names of the two levels of courts on the board along with key words.

Teach
- Can Disputes Be Resolved Privately? (p. 53)
- Different Levels of Courts (pp. 53-54)
- What's Your Verdict? (p. 53)

Apply
- Think About Legal Concepts 1-6 (p. 54)
- Think Critically About Evidence 7-10 (p. 54)

Assess
- Lesson 4-1 Quiz (Unit 1 Resource Book, p. 59)
- Reteach
  Have students set up a mock trial in the classroom.
- Enrich
  Have students create a graphic of a court scene.

Close
- Review questions in *What's Your Verdict?* on page 53.

Law for Business and Personal Use

Teacher: _____

Week of: _____

| M | T | W | Th | F |

Lesson 4-2   Federal Court System
Pages 55-57

Goals
- Identify the source of power of the federal courts
- Name the various levels of federal courts and describe their jurisdictions

Teaching Resources
LAW LEARNING PACKAGE
- Student Activities and Study Guide, pp. 21-22
- Transparencies 1, 8
- Unit 1 Resource Book, pp. 63-66
- Lesson 4-2 Spanish Resources

Focus
- Write "What is a federal court?" on the board. Discuss the answer.

Teach
- Origins of Our Federal Court System (p. 55)
- Jurisdiction of the Federal Courts (pp. 55-57)
- What's Your Verdict? (p. 55)
- Cultural Diversity in Law, *Sweden* (p. 56)
- Law and the Internet (p. 56)

Apply
- Think About Legal Concepts 1-5 (p. 57)
- Think Critically About Evidence 6-9 (p. 57)

Assess
- Lesson 4-2 Quiz (Unit 1 Resource Book, p. 63)
- Reteach
  Have students write three short paragraphs that explain the jurisdiction of each of the following courts: federal district courts, federal court of appeals, and the United States Supreme Court.
- Enrich
  Take students on a field trip to a federal court to witness a trial.

Close
- Have students make a poster or display of the federal court system diagram on page 56. Then have students add information on each of the courts.

Law for Business and Personal Use   Teacher: _____
                                                          Week of: _____
                                                              M   T   W   Th   F

Lesson 4-3   State Court Systems
Pages 58-61

Goals
- Compare the structure of a typical state court with the structure of the federal courts
- Identify typical state courts of specialized jurisdiction
- Discuss the jurisdiction of the various typical state courts

Teaching Resources
LAW LEARNING PACKAGE
- Student Activities and Study Guide, pp. 23-24
- Transparencies 1, 2
- Unit 1 Resource Book, pp. 67-70
- Lesson 4-3 Spanish Resources

Focus
- Write "What is the difference between a federal court and a state court?" on the board. Discuss the answer.

Teach
- Structure of State Court Systems (pp. 58-59)
- State Courts with Specialized Jurisdiction (pp. 59-60)
- What's Your Verdict? (p. 58, 59)
- A Question of Ethics (p. 60)
- FYI (p. 60)
- Curriculum Connection, *Social Studies* (TE, p. 59)
- Think Critically Through Visuals (TE, p. 60)

Apply
- Think About Legal Concepts 1-5 (p. 61)
- Think Critically About Evidence 6-10 (p. 61)

Assess
- Lesson 4-3 Quiz (Unit 1 Resource Book, p. 67)
- Reteach
  Have students work with peer tutors to write three questions about this chapter.
- Enrich
  Have students make a chart of your state court system.

Close
- Read and discuss *Prevent Legal Difficulties* on page 61.
- Have students work in pairs to write a one paragraph summary of the chapter.

Law for Business and Personal Use

Chapter 4 in Review
Pages 62-65

Teaching Resources
LAW LEARNING PACKAGE
* Chapter 4 Test (Unit 1 Resource Book, pp. 71-73)
* Interactive Business Law Study Guide Chapter 4
* WESTEST Chapter 4

Review
* Concepts in Brief 1-10 (p. 62)
* Your Legal Vocabulary 1-10 (p.62)
* Review Legal Concepts 11-14 (p. 62)
* Write About Legal Concepts 15-17 (p. 63)
* Think Critically About Evidence 18-23 (p. 63)
* Analyze Real Cases 24-29 (p. 64)

Apply
* Case for Legal Thinking (p. 65)
  * Practice Judging 1-3

Assess
* WESTEST Chapter 4
* Chapter 4 Test (Unit 1 Resource Book, pp. 71-73)

Law for Business and Personal Use

Chapter 5   Our Criminal Laws
pp. 66-77

Introduction
- Hot Debate (p. 66)

Chapter 5 Teaching Resources
LAW LEARNING PACKAGE
- Unit 1 Resource Book, pp. 77-87
- Transparencies 1, 2, 9, 10
- Student Activities and Study Guide, pp. 25-32
- Lessons 5-1 and 5-2 Spanish Resources
- Interactive Business Law Study Guide Chapter 5
- WESTEST Chapter 5

Law for Business and Personal Use   Teacher: _____
                                                       Week of: _____
                                                       M   T   W   Th   F

Lesson 5-1   Criminal Law
                       Pages 67-70

Goals
* Define the elements present in all crimes
* Describe crimes that commonly occur in the business environment

Teaching Resources
LAW LEARNING PACKAGE
* Student Activities and Study Guide, pp. 25-28
* Transparencies 1, 2, 9, 10
* Unit 1 Resource Book, pp. 77-80
* Lesson 5-1 Spanish Resources

Focus
* Write "What is a crime?" on the board. Discuss.
* Ask what the difference is between a crime and a civil offense.

Teach
* What Are Crimes? (pp. 67-68)
* Classification of Crimes (p. 68)
* Business-Related Crimes (pp. 69-70)
* What's Your Verdict? (pp. 67, 68, 69)
* A Question of Ethics (p. 68)
* In This Case (p. 70)
* Curriculum Connection, *Social Studies* (TE, p. 68)
* Curriculum Connection, *History* (TE, p. 69)
* Think Critically Through Visuals (TE, p. 69)

Apply
* Think About Legal Concepts 1-5 (p. 70)
* Think Critically About Evidence 6-8 (p. 70)

Assess
* Lesson 5-1 Quiz (Unit 1 Resource Book, p. 77)
* Reteach
  Use the graphic organizers created in this section. Make a copy for each student, omitting the words on the copy. Have students work in pairs to fill out the blocks with key words and information about each crime.
* Enrich
  Have students research the punishment in your state for each crime in the graphic organizer.

Close
* Have students create a graphic organizer of all business-related crimes.

Law for Business and Personal Use

Teacher: _____
Week of: _____

M   T   W   Th   F

Lesson 5-2   Criminal Procedure
Pages 71-73

Goals
- Know the rights a person has when arrested
- Recognize a person's potential criminal liability for the actions of others
- Understand the justifiability of the common defenses to criminal charges

Teaching Resources
LAW LEARNING PACKAGE
- Student Activities and Study Guide, pp. 29-32
- Transparency 1
- Unit 1 Resource Book, pp. 81-84
- Lesson 5-2 Spanish Resources

Focus
- Write "Why is it important for individuals to have protections from certain government actions?" on the board. Discuss.

Teach
- Rights and Responsibilities (pp. 71-72)
- Defenses to Criminal Charges (p. 72)
- Punishments for Crimes (pp. 72-73)
- What's Your Verdict? (p. 71-72)
- Cultural Diversity in Law, *France* (p. 71)

Apply
- Think About Legal Concepts 1-5 (p. 73)
- Think Critically About Evidence 6-10 (p. 73)

Assess
- Lesson 5-2 Quiz (Unit 1 Resource Book, p. 81)
- Reteach
  Create a mapping exercise. One the board have students take turns writing a word from this lesson. Then have the class add words around the original word. Do this for several words.
- Enrich
  Have students stage a mock crime, arrest, interrogation, and court scene.

Close
- Read and discuss *Prevent Legal Difficulties* on page 73.
- Have students work with a partner to make a list of vocabulary words in this section and then quiz each other on the definitions.

Law for Business and Personal Use

Chapter 5 in Review
Pages 74-77

Teaching Resources
LAW LEARNING PACKAGE
- Chapter 5 Test (Unit 1 Resource Book, pp. 85-87)
- Interactive Business Law Study Guide Chapter 5
- WESTEST Chapter 5

Review
- Concepts in Brief 1-8 (p. 74)
- Your Legal Vocabulary 1-12 (p. 74)
- Review Legal Concepts 13-15 (p. 75)
- Write About Legal Concepts 16-17 (p. 75)
- Think Critically About Evidence 18-21 (p. 75)
- Analyze Real Cases 22-28 (p. 76)

Apply
- Case for Legal Thinking (p. 77)
  - Practice Judging 1-4

Assess
- WESTEST Chapter 5
- Chapter 5 Test (Unit 1 Resource Book, pp. 85-87)

Law for Business and Personal Use

Teacher: _____

Week of: _____

| M | T | W | Th | F |

Chapter 6   Personal Injury Laws
pp. 78-95

Introduction
- Hot Debate (p. 78)

Chapter 6 Teaching Resources
LAW LEARNING PACKAGE
- Unit 1 Resource Book, pp. 91-104
- Transparencies 1, 2, 11
- Student Activities and Study Guide, pp. 39-40
- Lessons 6-1, 6-2, and 6-3 Spanish Resources
- Interactive Business Law Study Guide Chapter 6
- WESTEST Chapter 6

Law for Business and Personal Use

Teacher: _____

Week of: _____

M   T   W   Th   F

Lesson 6-1   Offenses Against Individuals
Pages 79-81

Goals
- Distinguish a crime from a tort
- Discuss the elements of a tort
- Explain when a person is responsible for another's tort

Teaching Resources

LAW LEARNING PACKAGE
- Student Activities and Study Guide, pp. 33-34
- Transparencies 1-11
- Unit 1 Resource Book, pp. 91-94
- Lesson 6-1 Spanish Resources

Focus
- Write "What is a tort?" on the board. Discuss the difference between a crime and a tort.

Teach
- How Do Crimes and Torts Differ? (p. 79)
- Elements of a Tort (pp. 79-80)
- Responsibility for the Torts of Another (p. 80)
- What's Your Verdict? (pp. 79-80)
- Think Critically Through Visuals (TE, p. 80)

Apply
- Think About Legal Concepts 1-9 (p. 81)
- Think Critically About Evidence 10-14 (p. 81)

Assess
- Lesson 6-1 Quiz (Unit 1 Resource Book, p. 91)
- Reteach
  Have students write the four common elements of a tort on the board. On another section of the board, write the definition for each element. Have students orally match the correct definition to each element.
- Enrich
  Have small groups of students write a scenario for one of the following: a tort only; a crime only; a tort and crime. Have various groups present their scenario to the class.

Close
- Have pairs of students create a graphic organizer comparing the elements of torts.

Law for Business and Personal Use

Teacher: _____
Week of: _____
        M   T   W   Th   F

Lesson 6-2   Common Intentional Torts
Pages 82-86

Goals
- Identify nine common intentional torts
- Define negligence and strict liability

Teaching Resources
LAW LEARNING PACKAGE
- Student Activities and Study Guide, pp. 35-38
- Transparencies 1, 2
- Unit 1 Resource Book, pp. 95-98
- Lesson 6-2 Spanish Resources

Focus
- Write "What is an intentional tort?" on the board. Discuss.

Teach
- Common Intentional Torts (pp. 82-84)
- What Is Negligence? (pp. 84-85)
- What Is Strict Liability? (pp. 85-86)
- What's Your Verdict? (pp. 82, 84, 85)
- In This Case (pp. 82, 83, 84, 85)
- A Question of Ethics (p. 83)
- FYI (p. 86)
- Curriculum Connection, *Language Arts* (TE, pp. 83, 85)
- Curriculum Connection, *Economics* (TE, p. 84)
- Think Critically Through Visuals (TE, pp. 84, 85)

Apply
- Think About Legal Concepts 1-7 (p. 86)
- Think Critically About Evidence 8-11 (p. 86)

Assess
- Lesson 6-2 Quiz (Unit 1 Resource Book, p. 95)
- Reteach
  Have pairs of students create a graphic organizer of the nine intentional torts.
- Enrich
  Have pairs of students use their graphic organizers to draw or create a design or picture that represents each of the nine intentional torts.

Close
- Review questions in *What's Your Verdict?* on pages 82 and 85.

Law for Business and Personal Use

Lesson 6-3   Civil Procedure
Pages 87-89

Goals
- Discuss what damages are available to victims of torts
- Explain the various stages of a civil suit

Teaching Resources
LAW LEARNING PACKAGE
- Student Activities and Study Guide, pp. 39-40
- Transparency 1
- Unit 1 Resource Book, pp. 99-102
- Lesson 6-3 Spanish Resources

Focus
- Write "What are damages?" on the board. Discuss.

Teach
- What Can a Tort Victim Collect? (p. 87)
- How Is a Civil Case Tried? (pp. 87-88)
- How Is a Judgment Satisfied? (p. 88)
- What's Your Verdict? (pp. 87, 88)
- In This Case (p. 88)
- Cultural Diversity in Law (TE, p. 88)
- Curriculum Connection, *Social Science* (TE, p. 88)

Apply
- Think About Legal Concepts 1-5 (p. 89)
- Think Critically About Evidence 6-8 (p. 89)

Assess
- Lesson 6-3 Quiz (Unit 1 Resource Book, p. 99)
- Reteach
  Have students work with a peer tutor to write one-paragraph answers to these questions: What kind of offense is a tort? What can a tort victim collect? How is a civil case tried? How is a judgment satisfied?
- Enrich
  Have students role-play a civil court case that involves a tort.

Close
- Read and discuss *Prevent Legal Difficulties* on page 89.
- Review questions in *What's Your Verdict?* on pages 87 and 88.

Law for Business and Personal Use

Chapter 6 in Review
Pages 90-93

Teaching Resources
LAW LEARNING PACKAGE
- Chapter 6 Test (Unit 1 Resource Book, pp. 103-104)
- Interactive Business Law Study Guide Chapter 6
- WESTEST Chapter 6

Review
- Concepts in Brief 1-6 (p. 90)
- Your Legal Vocabulary 1-14 (p.90)
- Review Legal Concepts 15-18 (p. 91)
- Write About Legal Concepts 19-20 (p. 91)
- Think Critically About Evidence 21-24 (p. 91)
- Analyze Real Cases 25-30 (p. 92)

Apply
- Case for Legal Thinking (p. 93)
  - Practice Judging 1-2

Assess
- WESTEST Chapter 6
- Chapter 6 Test (Unit 1 Resource Book, pp. 103-104)

Unit 1 Law, Justice, and You   (Chapters 1-6)
pp. 2-95
Wrap-Up
- Entrepreneurs and the Law (pp. 94-95)
  - Project 1 Law, Justice, and You
  - Think Critically Through Visuals (TE, p. 95)

Law for Business and Personal Use   Teacher: _____
                                                 Week of: _____
                                                          M   T   W   Th   F

Unit 2   Fundamentals of Contracts (Chapters 7-14)
pp. 96-211
Introduction
In Practice Profile: Gail Hallock, Legal Secretary (p. 97)

Chapter 7   Offer and Acceptance
pp. 98-113
Introduction
•   Hot Debate (p. 98)

Chapter 7 Teaching Resources
LAW LEARNING PACKAGE
•   Unit 2 Resource Book, pp. 5-18
•   Transparencies 1, 2, 13
•   Student Activities and Study Guide, pp. 41-46
•   Lessons 7-1, 7-2, and 7-3 Spanish Resources
•   Interactive Business Law Study Guide Chapter 7
•   WESTEST Chapter 7

Law for Business and Personal Use

Teacher: _____
Week of: _____
       M   T   W   Th   F

Lesson 7-1   Creation of Offers
Pages 99-102

Goals
- List the elements required to form a contract
- Describe the requirements of an offer

Teaching Resources
LAW LEARNING PACKAGE
- Student Activities and Study Guide, pp. 41-42
- Transparencies 1, 2, 13
- Unit 2 Resource Book, pp. 5-8
- Lesson 7-1 Spanish Resources

Focus
- Ask these questions:
  - What distinguishes a contract from other agreements?
  - What two actions are necessary to form an agreement which may result in a contract?
  - Do contracts require particular language?

Teach
- What Is a Contract? (p. 99)
- Requirements of an Offer (pp. 100-102)
- What's Your Verdict? (p. 99, 100)
- In This Case (p. 100)
- A Question of Ethics (p. 101)
- Curriculum Connection, *History* (TE, p. 100)
- Think Critically Through Visuals (TE, p. 101)

Apply
- Think About Legal Concepts 1-9 (p. 102)
- Think Critically About Evidence 10-13 (p. 102)

Assess
- Lesson 7-1 Quiz (Unit 2 Resource Book, p. 5)
- Reteach
  Have students summarize in writing the three requirements of a valid offer.
- Enrich
  Videotape one or more television commercials. Show the clips and ask students to identify the words that make the commercials appear to be either offers or invitations to make offers.

Close
- Review lesson goals on page 99. Make sure students can meet these goals.

Law for Business and Personal Use   Teacher: _____
                                                       Week of: _____
                                                                M   T   W   Th   F

Lesson 7-2   Termination of Offers
Pages 103-105

Goals
- Describe how an offeror can end an offer
- Tell how an offeree can end an offer
- Explain how the parties can create offers that cannot be ended by the offeror

Teaching Resources
LAW LEARNING PACKAGE
- Student Activities and Study Guide, pp. 43-44
- Transparency 1
- Unit 2 Resource Book, pp. 9-12
- Lesson 7-2 Spanish Resources

Focus
- Ask students whether they think offers to contract might be terminated at different times depending on the subject matter of the offer. Discuss.

Teach
- How Can Offers Be Ended? (pp. 103-104)
- How Can an Offer Be Kept Open? (p. 104)
- What's Your Verdict? (pp. 103, 104)
- In This Case (p. 104)
- Curriculum Connection, *Communications* (TE, p. 104)
- Think Critically Through Visuals (TE, p. 104)

Apply
- Think About Legal Concepts 1-11 (p. 105)
- Think Critically About Evidence 12-15 (p. 105)

Assess
- Lesson 7-2 Quiz (Unit 2 Resource Book, p. 9)
- Reteach
  Have pairs of student outline six ways an offer can be ended.
- Enrich
  Have pairs of students write a one-page provision on how to keep an offer open for the Uniform Commercial Code (UCC)

Close
- Review lesson goals on page 103. Make sure students can meet these goals.

Law for Business and Personal Use

Teacher: _____

Week of: _____

M   T   W   Th   F

Lesson 7-3   Acceptances
Pages 106-109

Goals
- Discuss the requirements of an effective acceptance
- Determine at what point in time an acceptance is effective

Teaching Resources
LAW LEARNING PACKAGE
- Student Activities and Study Guide, pp. 45-46
- Transparency 1
- Unit 2 Resource Book, pp. 13-16
- Lesson 7-3 Spanish Resources

Focus
- Read and discuss the following scenario.
  - John makes an offer to Paul. Paul is not interested, but Paul's friend, who was standing nearby, hears the offer and says she accepts. Has a contract been formed?

Teach
- How Are Acceptances Created? (pp. 106-108)
- What's Your Verdict? (p. 106)
- Cultural Diversity in Law, *Spain* (p. 107)
- In This Case (pp. 106, 107)
- Curriculum Connection, *Language Arts* (TE, p. 107)
- Think Critically Through Visuals (TE, p. 108)

Apply
- Think About Legal Concepts 1-5 (p. 108)
- Think Critically About Evidence 6-10 (p. 109)

Assess
- Lesson 7-3 Quiz (Unit 2 Resource Book, p. 13)
- Reteach
  Review and discuss each of the *In This Case* studies on pages 106-107.
- Enrich
  Have students brainstorm examples of unilateral contracts and bilateral contracts in everyday life.
  Have small groups of students each draw a cartoon to illustrate a principle taught in this lesson.

Close
- Read and discuss *Prevent Legal Difficulties* on page 109.

Law for Business and Personal Use

Chapter 7 in Review
Pages 110-113

Teaching Resources
LAW LEARNING PACKAGE
- Chapter 7 Test (Unit 2 Resource Book, pp. 17-18)
- Interactive Business Law Study Guide Chapter 7
- WESTEST Chapter 7

Review
- Concepts in Brief 1-9 (p. 110)
- Your Legal Vocabulary 1-10 (p.110)
- Review Legal Concepts 11-13 (p. 111)
- Write About Legal Concepts 14-16 (p. 111)
- Think Critically About Evidence 17-19 (p. 111)
- Analyze Real Cases 20-24 (p. 112)

Apply
- Case for Legal Thinking (p. 113)
  - Practice Judging 1-2

Assess
- WESTEST Chapter 7
- Chapter 7 Test (Unit 2 Resource Book, pp. 17-18)

Law for Business and Personal Use

Teacher: _____

Week of: _____

M   T   W   Th   F

Chapter 8   Genuine Agreement
pp. 114-127

Introduction
- Hot Debate (p. 114)

Chapter 8 Teaching Resources
LAW LEARNING PACKAGE
- Unit 2 Resource Book, pp. 23-32
- Transparencies 1, 2, 14
- Student Activities and Study Guide, pp. 47-52
- Lessons 8-1 and 8-2 Spanish Resources
- Interactive Business Law Study Guide Chapter 8
- WESTEST Chapter 8

Law for Business and Personal Use

Teacher: _____

Week of: _____

M   T   W   Th   F

Lesson 8-1   Duress and Undue Influence
Pages 115-118

Goals
* Define genuine agreement and rescission
* Identify when duress occurs
* Describe how someone may exercise undue influence

Teaching Resources
LAW LEARNING PACKAGE
* Student Activities and Study Guide, pp. 47-48
* Transparencies 1, 2
* Unit 2 Resource Book, pp. 23-26
* Lesson 8-1 Spanish Resources

Focus
* Discuss the following example:
    * The Thompsons were told by a man that if they did not sign a contract to repay a $2,000 loan at 40 percent interest, their son would be in danger of physical harm. Afraid that the threat would be carried out, the Thompsons signed the contract. Is the contract enforceable? Why or why not?

Teach
* Genuine Agreement and Rescission (pp. 115-117)
* What is Undue Influence? (p. 117)
* What's Your Verdict? (pp. 115, 117)
* In This Case (pp. 115, 117)
* A Question of Ethics (p. 115)
* Law in the Media (p. 116)
* Curriculum Connection, *Communication* (TE, p. 117)
* Think Critically Through Visuals (TE, p. 117)

Apply
* Think About Legal Concepts 1-11 (p. 118)
* Think Critically About Evidence 12-15 (p. 118)

Assess
* Lesson 8-1 Quiz (Unit 2 Resource Book, p. 23)
* Reteach
  Have students create a chart comparing duress and undue influence and the effect of each type of behavior on the resulting contract.
* Enrich
  Have students review the material presented in Chapters 5 and 6 on crimes and torts and relate it to the material presented in Lesson 8-1 on duress.

Close
* Review lesson goals on page 115. Make sure students can meet these goals.

Law for Business and Personal Use   Teacher: _____

                                                    Week of: _____
                                                    M   T   W   Th   F

Lesson 8-2   Mistake, Misrepresentation, and Fraud
                     Pages 119-123

Goals
- Describe the kinds of mistakes that can make a contract void or voidable
- Determine when misrepresentation has occurred
- Identify when fraud has occurred
- Discuss the remedies for mistake, misrepresentation, and fraud

Teaching Resources
LAW LEARNING PACKAGE
- Student Activities and Study Guide, pp. 49-52
- Transparencies 1, 14
- Unit 2 Resource Book, pp. 27-30
- Lesson 8-2 Spanish Resources

Focus
- Read and discuss the following example:
  - Jane contracts with Mike to purchase one of his two skateboards. Jane thinks she has bought the red one, a premier skateboard. Mike thinks Jane has bought the blue one, his less valuable skateboard. Does a contract exist?

Teach
- What Is a Unilateral Mistake? (p. 119)
- What Are Mutual Mistakes? (p. 120)
- What Is Misrepresentation? (pp. 120-121)
- Fraud and Remedies for Fraud (p. 122)
- What's Your Verdict? (pp. 119, 120, 122)
- Cultural Diversity in Law, *China* (p. 121)
- In This Case (pp. 119, 120)
- Curriculum Connection, *Language Arts/Drama* (TE, p. 120)
- Think Critically Through Visuals (TE, pp. 120, 122)

Apply
- Think About Legal Concepts 1-6 (p. 123)
- Think Critically About Evidence 7-10 (p. 123)

Assess
- Lesson 8-2 Quiz (Unit 2 Resource Book, p. 27)
- Reteach
  Have students find and discuss five examples of fact versus personal opinion in classified ads.
- Enrich
  Distribute sample contracts, such as insurance policies, car rental forms, or credit card applications. Have students read the contracts and list questions they would ask before signing the contract.

Close
- Read and discuss *Prevent Legal Difficulties* on page 123.
- Review questions in *What's Your Verdict?* on pages 119, 120, and 122..
- Review lesson goals on page 119. Make sure students can meet these goals.

Law for Business and Personal Use

Chapter 8 in Review
Pages 124-127

Teaching Resources
LAW LEARNING PACKAGE
- Chapter 8 Test (Unit 2 Resource Book, pp. 31-32)
- Interactive Business Law Study Guide Chapter 8
- WESTEST Chapter 8

Review
- Concepts in Brief 1-9 (p. 124)
- Your Legal Vocabulary 1-9 (p.124)
- Review Legal Concepts 10-15 (p. 125)
- Write About Legal Concepts 16-19 (p. 125)
- Think Critically About Evidence 20-23 (p. 125)
- Analyze Real Cases 24-28 (p. 126)

Apply
- Case for Legal Thinking (p. 127)
  - Practice Judging 1-3

Assess
- WESTEST Chapter 8
- Chapter 8 Test (Unit 2 Resource Book, pp. 31-32)

Law for Business and Personal Use

Chapter 9   Mutual Consideration
pp. 128-141

Introduction
- Hot Debate (p. 128)

Chapter 9 Teaching Resources
LAW LEARNING PACKAGE
- Unit 2 Resource Book, pp. 37-50
- Transparencies 1, 2
- Student Activities and Study Guide, pp. 53-60
- Lessons 9-1, 9-2, and 9-3 Spanish Resources
- Interactive Business Law Study Guide Chapter 9
- WESTEST Chapter 9

Law for Business and Personal Use

Lesson 9-1   What Is Consideration?
Pages 129-131

Goals
- Define consideration
- Determine when there is no consideration

Teaching Resources
LAW LEARNING PACKAGE
- Student Activities and Study Guide, pp. 53-54
- Transparency 1
- Unit 2 Resource Book, pp. 37-50
- Lesson 9-1 Spanish Resources

Focus
- Write the following on the board: "Identify five things you have made agreements to buy, sell, or do."
- Discuss students' lists of agreements.

Teach
- Consideration (pp. 129-131)
- What's Your Verdict? (p. 129)
- Cultural Diversity in Law, *England* (p. 131)
- In This Case (p. 130)
- Law and the Internet (p. 129)
- Curriculum Connection, *Communication* (TE, p. 130)

Apply
- Think About Legal Concepts 1-7 (p. 131)
- Think Critically About Evidence 8-10 (p. 131)

Assess
- Lesson 9-1 Quiz (Unit 2 Resource Book, p. 37)
- Reteach
  Have students work in small groups to create a poster illustrating one of the six types of consideration.
- Enrich
  Have students write two examples of verbal agreements, noting what consideration is given and received.

Close
- Bring several types of contracts to class. Have students work in groups to identify the consideration given and received in each contract. Make a chart of the results.

Law for Business and Personal Use

Teacher: _____

Week of: _____

M	T	W	Th	F

Lesson 9-2   Legal Value and Bargained-For Exchange
Pages 132-134

Goals
- Identify when there is legal value
- Determine when there is a bargained-for exchange

Teaching Resources
LAW LEARNING PACKAGE
- Student Activities and Study Guide, pp. 55-56
- Transparencies 1, 2
- Unit 2 Resource Book, pp. 41-44
- Lesson 9-2 Spanish Resources

Focus
- Read and discuss the following situation.
    - Ms. Miller, a high school government teacher, says to her students, "All of you have worked hard, and if you continue to perform at this level, I'll pay for a pizza party for the class at the end of the year--if I think it is warranted." The students continue to work hard, and class grades are high, but no party is given. Can the students enforce the promise?

Teach
- Legal Value (pp. 132-133)
- Bargained-For Exchange (p. 134)
- What's Your Verdict? (pp. 132, 134)
- In This Case (p. 133)
- A Question of Ethics (p. 133)
- Curriculum Connection, *Communication* (TE, p. 133)
- Think Critically Through Visuals (TE, p. 132)

Apply
- Think About Legal Concepts 1-7 (p. 134)
- Think Critically About Evidence 8-11 (p. 134)

Assess
- Lesson 9-2 Quiz (Unit 2 Resource Book, p. 41)
- Reteach
  Have students give some examples of past consideration related to school or home. Discuss.
  Have students give an example of an illusory promise. Discuss.
- Enrich
  Have students work in groups to create comic strip stories that illustrate a payment problem and how its settlement involved either an accord and satisfaction or a composition of creditors.

Close
- Review questions in *What's Your Verdict?* on pages 132 and 134.

Law for Business and Personal Use

Teacher: _____

Week of: _____

M   T   W   Th   F

Lesson 9-3   When Is Consideration Not Required?
Pages 135-137

Goals
- Identify when promissory estoppel applies
- Discuss situations in which consideration is not needed

Teaching Resources
LAW LEARNING PACKAGE
- Student Activities and Study Guide, pp. 59-60
- Transparency 1
- Unit 2 Resource Book, pp. 45-48
- Lesson 9-3 Spanish Resources

Focus
- Write "promissory" and "estoppel" on the board. Define each term.
- Ask students what they think a doctrine called "promissory estoppel" might mean.

Teach
- Promissory Estoppel (p. 135)
- Exceptions to the Consideration Requirement (pp. 135-136)
- What's Your Verdict? (p. 135)
- In This Case (p. 135)
- Curriculum Connection, *Math* (TE, p. 135)
- Think Critically Through Visuals (TE, p. 136)

Apply
- Think About Legal Concepts 1-8 (p. 136)
- Think Critically About Evidence 9-12 (p. 137)

Assess
- Lesson 9-3 Quiz (Unit 2 Resource Book, p. 45)
- Reteach
  Have students find exceptions to the requirement of mutual consideration in the material on pages 135-136.
- Enrich
  Have students make pledge cards for fund-raising events sponsored by school groups. The cards should include the name of the organization, what the funds will be used for, a space for the amount of the pledge, and a space for how and when the pledge will be paid.

Close
- Read and discuss *Prevent Legal Difficulties* on page 137.

Law for Business and Personal Use

Teacher: _____

Week of: _____

M   T   W   Th   F

Chapter 9 in Review
Pages 138-141

Teaching Resources

LAW LEARNING PACKAGE
- Chapter 9 Test (Unit 2 Resource Book, pp. 49-50)
- Interactive Business Law Study Guide Chapter 9
- WESTEST Chapter 9

Review
- Concepts in Brief 1-8 (p. 138)
- Your Legal Vocabulary 1-11 (p.138)
- Review Legal Concepts 12-15 (p. 139)
- Write About Legal Concepts 16-18 (p. 139)
- Think Critically About Evidence 19-23 (p. 139)
- Analyze Real Cases 24-28 (p. 140)

Apply
- Case for Legal Thinking (p. 141)
  - Practice Judging 1-3

Assess
- WESTEST Chapter 9
- Chapter 9 Test (Unit 2 Resource Book, pp. 49-50)

Law for Business and Personal Use

Chapter 10   Law of Capacity
pp. 142-153

Introduction
- Hot Debate (p. 142)

Chapter 10 Teaching Resources
LAW LEARNING PACKAGE
- Unit 2 Resource Book, pp. 55-64
- Transparencies 1, 2, 15, 16
- Student Activities and Study Guide, pp. 61-66
- Lessons 10-1 and 10-2 Spanish Resources
- Interactive Business Law Study Guide Chapter 10
- WESTEST Chapter 10

Law for Business and Personal Use   Teacher: _____

                                                     Week of: _____
                                                          M   T   W   Th   F

Lesson 10-1   Capacity Rights
Pages 143-146

Goals
- Identify parties who have contractual capacity
- Identify what contracts can be disaffirmed
- Explain the role of capacity in organizations

Teaching Resources
LAW LEARNING PACKAGE
- Student Activities and Study Guide, pp. 61-64
- Transparencies 1, 2, 15, 16
- Unit 2 Resource Book, pp. 55-58
- Lesson 10-1 Spanish Resources

Focus
- Ask students if they have ever tried to disaffirm a contract. Point out that if the right of disaffirmance did not exist, there would probably be many cases of exploitation of minors in contracts with adults.

Teach
- What Is Capacity? (pp. 143-144)
- Which Contracts Can Be Disaffirmed? (p. 145)
- Capacity in Organizations (pp. 145-146)
- What's Your Verdict? (pp. 143, 145)
- Cultural Diversity in Law, *Early America* (p. 144)
- In This Case (p. 144)
- A Question of Ethics (p. 146)
- Curriculum Connection, *Social Studies* (TE, p. 144)
- Think Critically Through Visuals (TE, pp. 143, 145)

Apply
- Think About Legal Concepts 1-7 (p. 146)
- Think Critically About Evidence 8-10 (p. 146)

Assess
- Lesson 10-1 Quiz (Unit 2 Resource Book, p. 55)
- Reteach
  Have students work together to create an outline of this lesson.
- Enrich
  On index cards, write scenarios that depict enforceable and unenforceable contacts involving minors or others lacking contractual capacity. Have various small groups of students improvise skits based on the situation on the card they draw or are given.

Close
- Review lesson goals on page 143. Make sure students can meet these goals.

Law for Business and Personal Use   Teacher: _____
                                                          Week of: _____
                                                                   M   T   W   Th   F

Lesson 10-2   Limitations on Capacity Rights
Pages 147-149

Goals
- Identify the time when a contract cannot be disaffirmed
- Identify contracts that cannot be disaffirmed
- Explain the consequences of misrepresenting age

Teaching Resources
LAW LEARNING PACKAGE
- Student Activities and Study Guide, pp. 65-66
- Transparency 1
- Unit 2 Resource Book, pp. 59-62
- Lesson 10-2 Spanish Resources

Focus
- Read the following quote from Benjamin Cardozo, Associate Justice of the U.S. Supreme Court, 1932-1938. "Liberty of contract is not an absolute concept. It is relative to many conditions of time and place and circumstance." Discuss.

Teach
- Time of Disaffirmance and Ratification (p. 147)
- Return of Goods or Services (p. 147)
- Which Contracts Cannot Be Disaffirmed? (p. 148)
- Misrepresenting Your Age (pp. 148-149)
- What's Your Verdict? (pp. 147-148)
- Curriculum Connection, *Communication* (TE, p. 147)
- Think Critically Through Visuals (TE, p. 148)

Apply
- Think About Legal Concepts 1-6 (p. 149)
- Think Critically About Evidence 7-10 (p. 149)

Assess
- Lesson 10-2 Quiz (Unit 2 Resource Book, p. 59)
- Reteach
  Have weak students work with peer tutors to review the material covered in this lesson. The peer tutor should provide examples of each concept as necessary.
- Enrich
  Have small groups of students write and record a song, rap, or poem called, "Warning! You're Not Too Young," warning other minors about contracts that cannot be disaffirmed because of their age. Play the recordings for the class.

Close
- Read and discuss *Prevent Legal Difficulties* on page 149.
- Read the main headings within the lesson and have students write a couple of sentences summarizing the content of each section.

Law for Business and Personal Use

Chapter 10 in Review
Pages 150-153

Teaching Resources
LAW LEARNING PACKAGE
- Chapter 10 Test (Unit 2 Resource Book, pp. 63-64)
- Interactive Business Law Study Guide Chapter 10
- WESTEST Chapter 10

Review
- Concepts in Brief 1-10 (p. 150)
- Your Legal Vocabulary 1-12 (p.150)
- Review Legal Concepts 13-17 (p. 151)
- Write About Legal Concepts 18-21 (p. 151)
- Think Critically About Evidence 22-25 (p. 151)
- Analyze Real Cases 26-29 (p. 152)

Apply
- Case for Legal Thinking (p. 153)
    - Practice Judging 1-3

Assess
- WESTEST Chapter 10
- Chapter 10 Test (Unit 2 Resource Book, pp. 63-64)

Law for Business and Personal Use

Chapter 11   LEGALITY OF CONTRACTS
pp. 154-165

Introduction

- Hot Debate (p. 154)

Chapter 11 Teaching Resources

LAW LEARNING PACKAGE

- Unit 2 Resource Book, pp. 66-75
- Transparencies 1, 2
- Student Activities and Study Guide, pp. 67-72
- Lessons 11-1 and 11-2 Spanish Resources
- Interactive Business Law Study Guide Chapter 11
- WESTEST Chapter 11

Law for Business and Personal Use   Teacher: _____

Week of: _____

M   T   W   Th   F

Lesson 11-1   Which Agreements Are Illegal
Pages 155-158

Goals
- Describe general features of contracts which make them illegal
- Describe particular illegal contracts

Teaching Resources
LAW LEARNING PACKAGE
- Student Activities and Study Guide, pp. 67-70
- Transparency 1
- Unit 2 Resource Book, pp. 66-69
- Lesson 11-1 Spanish Resources

Focus
- State that courts generally hope to enforce contracts. Ask students if they can think of situations in which contracts cannot or should not be enforced, even if the parties have agreed and there is consideration. Introduce the topic of illegal agreements.

Teach
- Illegal Agreements (pp. 155-158)
- What's Your Verdict? (p. 155)
- Cultural Diversity in Law, *Native Americans* (p. 156)
- In This Case (pp. 156, 157)
- Curriculum Connection, *Math* (TE, p. 156)
- Think Critically Through Visuals (TE, p. 157)

Apply
- Think About Legal Concepts 1-6 (p. 158)
- Think Critically About Evidence 7-9 (p. 158)

Assess
- Lesson 11-1 Quiz (Unit 2 Resource Book, p. 66)
- Reteach
  Display the transparency you created for the Teach activity on page 155. Revealing only one illegal agreement at a time, have students review orally what they have learned about it.
- Enrich
  Have students clip, label, and display newspaper or magazine articles relating to illegal agreements.

Close
- Review lesson goals on page 155. Make sure students can meet these goals.

Law for Business and Personal Use

Teacher: _____

Week of: _____

M   T   W   Th   F

Lesson 11-2   Enforceability of Illegal Agreements
Pages 159-161

Goals
- Describe how courts help parties to illegal contracts under the common law
- Describe how courts help parties to illegal contracts under the UCC

Teaching Resources

LAW LEARNING PACKAGE
- Student Activities and Study Guide, pp. 71-72
- Transparencies 1, 2
- Unit 2 Resource Book, pp. 70-73
- Lesson 11-2 Spanish Resources

Focus
- Have students discuss the following problem in small groups.
  - A welfare recipient with a fourth-grade education agrees to purchase a refrigerator for $2,300. He signs a two-year installment contract with a high but legal interest rate. The same type of refrigerator usually sells for $500 on the market. Is it possible that this contract is unconscionable?

Teach
- How Do Courts Treat Parties to Illegal Contracts? (pp. 159-160)
- What's Your Verdict? (p. 159)
- In This Case (pp. 159, 160)
- A Question of Ethics (p. 160)
- Curriculum Connection, *Communications* (TE, p. 160)

Apply
- Think About Legal Concepts 1-4 (p. 161)
- Think Critically About Evidence 5-7 (p. 161)

Assess
- Lesson 11-2 Quiz (Unit 2 Resource Book, p. 70)
- Reteach
  Have students outline the lesson.
- Enrich
  Have pairs of students role-play scenarios between someone trying to create an illegal agreement and an innocent party.

Close
- Read and discuss Prevent Legal Difficulties on page 161.
- Have each student jot down a scenario that contains a combination of legal and illegal provisions.

Law for Business and Personal Use

Teacher: _____
Week of: _____
        M   T   W   Th   F

Chapter 11 in Review
Pages 162-165

Teaching Resources
LAW LEARNING PACKAGE
- Chapter 11 Test (Unit 2 Resource Book, pp. 74-75)
- Interactive Business Law Study Guide Chapter 11
- WESTEST Chapter 11

Review
- Concepts in Brief 1-3 (p. 162)
- Your Legal Vocabulary 1-14 (p. 162)
- Review Legal Concepts 15-18 (p. 163)
- Write About Legal Concepts 19-23 (p. 163)
- Think Critically About Evidence 24-27 (p. 163)
- Analyze Real Cases 28-34 (p. 164)

Apply
- Case for Legal Thinking (p. 165)
  - Practice Judging 1-2

Assess
- WESTEST Chapter 11
- Chapter 11 Test (Unit 2 Resource Book, pp. 74-75)

Law for Business and Personal Use

Chapter 12   Written Contracts
pp. 166-181

Introduction
• Hot Debate (p. 166)

Chapter 12 Teaching Resources
LAW LEARNING PACKAGE
• Unit 2 Resource Book, pp. 79-93
• Transparencies 1, 2, 17, 18
• Student Activities and Study Guide, pp. 73-80
• Lessons 12-1, 12-2, and 12-3 Spanish Resources
• Interactive Business Law Study Guide Chapter 12
• WESTEST Chapter 12

Law for Business and Personal Use

Teacher: _____

Week of: _____

M   T   W   Th   F

Lesson 12-1   What Is the Statute of Frauds?
Pages 167-170

Goals
- Describe the statue of frauds
- Discuss the consequences of failure to comply with the statute
- Describe what writing satisfies the statute under the common law and the UCC
- Explain how the signature influences enforcement of contracts

Teaching Resources
LAW LEARNING PACKAGE
- Student Activities and Study Guide, pp. 73-76
- Transparencies 1, 17
- Unit 2 Resource Book, pp. 79-82
- Lesson 12-1 Spanish Resources

Focus
- Write "Must all contracts be in writing?" on the board. Discuss.

Teach
- Must All Contracts Be in Writing? (p. 167)
- What Is the Statute of Frauds? (pp. 168-169)
- What Writing Does the Statute Require? (pp. 169-170)
- What's Your Verdict? (pp. 167, 168, 169)
- Cultural Diversity in Law, *International* (p. 168)
- In This Case (pp. 167, 168, 169)
- Curriculum Connection, *Communication* (TE, p. 169)
- Think Critically Through Visuals (TE, p. 168)

Apply
- Think About Legal Concepts 1-8 (p. 170)
- Think Critically About Evidence 9-11 (p. 170)

Assess
- Lesson 12-1 Quiz (Unit 2 Resource Book, p. 79)
- Reteach
  Have students skim the section, What Is the Statute of Frauds, and note the arguments given for putting a contract in writing.
- Enrich
  Have students discuss reasons why people might purposefully avoid using a written agreement.

Close
- Review the *In This Case* example on page 169.

Law for Business and Personal Use

Teacher: _____

Week of: _____

Lesson 12-2   Contracts Within and Exceptions to the Statute of Frauds
Pages 171-173

Goals
* Identify those contracts which are within the statute of frauds
* Describe exceptions where contracts within the statute need not be in writing to be enforced

Teaching Resources
LAW LEARNING PACKAGE
* Student Activities and Study Guide, pp. 77-78
* Transparency 1
* Unit 2 Resource Book, pp. 83-86
* Lesson 12-2 Spanish Resources

Focus
* Write "within the statute of frauds" on the board. Have students review the text concerning the five types of executory contracts that must be evidenced by a writing and signed by the other party.

Teach
* What Contracts Are Within the Statute of Frauds? (pp. 171-173)
* What's Your Verdict? (p. 171)
* In This Case (pp. 171, 172, 173)
* Curriculum Connection, *Social Studies* (TE, p. 172)

Apply
* Think About Legal Concepts 1-4 (p. 173)
* Think Critically About Evidence 5-7 (p. 173)

Assess
* Lesson 12-2 Quiz (Unit 2 Resource Book, p. 83)
* Reteach
  Ask students whether each situation is subject to the statute of frauds. Include business situations, such as selling a car, selling a lot of commercial property, and contracting for telephone service.
* Enrich
  Have students work in small groups to list five to ten examples of informal situations that involve a person assuming the legal or financial obligations of another.

Close
* Review the five *In This* Case examples in the lesson. Make sure students understand how each applies to a specific contract requiring a writing.

Law for Business and Personal Use   Teacher: _____
                                                       Week of: _____
                                                       M   T   W   Th   F

Lesson 12-3   How Are Contracts Interpreted?
Pages 174-177

Goals
- Describe how conflicting oral and written communications are reconciled
- Explain how conflicts among written elements in a contract are reconciled

Teaching Resources
LAW LEARNING PACKAGE
- Student Activities and Study Guide, pp. 79-80
- Transparencies 1, 2, 18
- Unit 2 Resource Book, pp. 87-90
- Lesson 12-3 Spanish Resources

Focus
- Write "What is the parol evidence rule?" on the board. Discuss.

Teach
- What Is the Parol Evidence Rule? (p. 174)
- How Are Conflicts in Written Terms Interpreted? (p. 175)
- What's Your Verdict? (pp. 174, 175)
- A Question of Ethics (p. 176)
- Curriculum Connection, *Communication* (TE, p. 176)
- Think Critically Through Visuals (TE, p. 175)

Apply
- Think About Legal Concepts 1-8 (p. 176)
- Think Critically About Evidence 9-12 (p. 177)

Assess
- Lesson 12-3 Quiz (Unit 2 Resource Book, p. 87)
- Reteach
  Have pairs of students create and role-play a situation involving a contract based, in part, on parol evidence.
- Enrich
  Have students brainstorm wise consumer rules for entering into contracts. Then have students collaborate to create a poster illustrating these rules.

Close
- Read and discuss *Prevent Legal Difficulties* on page 177.

Law for Business and Personal Use

Teacher: _____

Week of: _____

M   T   W   Th   F

Chapter 12 in Review
Pages 178-181

Teaching Resources
LAW LEARNING PACKAGE
- Chapter 12 Test (Unit 2 Resource Book, pp. 91-93)
- Interactive Business Law Study Guide Chapter 12
- WESTEST Chapter 12

Review
- Concepts in Brief 1-7 (p. 178)
- Your Legal Vocabulary 1-10 (p. 178)
- Review Legal Concepts 11-14 (p. 179)
- Write About Legal Concepts 15-18 (p. 179)
- Think Critically About Evidence 19-24 (p. 179)
- Analyze Real Cases 25-28 (p. 180)

Apply
- Case for Legal Thinking (p. 181)
  - Practice Judging 1-2

Assess
- WESTEST Chapter 12
- Chapter 12 Test (Unit 2 Resource Book, pp. 91-93)

Law for Business and Personal Use

Chapter 13   Contractual Duties
pp. 182-195

Introduction

- Hot Debate (p. 182)

Chapter 13 Teaching Resources

- LAW LEARNING PACKAGE
  - Unit 2 Resource Book, pp. 98-108
  - Transparencies 1, 2, 19
  - Student Activities and Study Guide, pp. 81-86
  - Lessons 13-1 and 13-2 Spanish Resources
  - Interactive Business Law Study Guide Chapter 13
  - WESTEST Chapter 13

Law for Business and Personal Use

Teacher: _____

Week of: _____

M   T   W   Th   F

Lesson 13-1   Transfer of Contractual Obligations
Pages 183-185

Goals
- Describe which rights can be assigned
- Identify what duties can be delegated

Teaching Resources
LAW LEARNING PACKAGE
- Student Activities and Study Guide, pp. 81-82
- Transparency 1
- Unit 2 Resource Book, pp. 98-101
- Lesson 13-1 Spanish Resources

Focus
- Ask "Into what kinds of contracts have you entered?"
- Ask "What acts or terms might legally end such contracts?"

Teach
- Assigning Contractual Rights (pp. 183-184)
- Delegating Contractual Duties (p. 184)
- What Are the Obligations of Obligors? (pp. 184-185)
- What's Your Verdict? (pp. 183, 184)
- In This Case (pp. 183, 184)
- Think Critically Through Visuals (TE, pp. 183, 184)

Apply
- Think About Legal Concepts 1-5 (p. 185)
- Think Critically About Evidence 6-9 (p. 185)

Assess
- Lesson 13-1 Quiz (Unit 2 Resource Book, p. 101)
- Reteach
  Have students identify the five contractual rights that may not be transferred because performance would be changed in important ways.
- Enrich
  Have students make up three examples of each of the five contractual rights that may not be transferred because performance would be changed in important ways. Each example should be written on an index card. Have students work in pairs, taking turns drawing cards and categorizing each example.

Close
- Review the *In This Case* on page 184. Ask students to identify the obligor, the assignor, and the assignee.

Law for Business and Personal Use   Teacher: _____

                                                       Week of: _____
                                                       M   T   W   Th   F

Lesson 13-2   Performance of Duties
Pages 186-189

Goals
- Describe how contracts are usually satisfied
- Explain the ways contracts can be discharged other than by performance of their terms

Teaching Resources
LAW LEARNING PACKAGE
- Student Activities and Study Guide, pp. 83-86
- Transparencies 1, 2, 19
- Unit 2 Resource Book, pp. 102-105
- Lesson 13-2 Spanish Resources

Focus
- Write "How are contracts usually discharged?" on the board.
- List the following on the board: "1. complete performance; 2. substantial performance"

Teach
- How Are Contracts Usually Discharged? (pp. 186-187)
- How Else Can Contracts Be Discharged? (pp. 187-190)
- What Is the Effect of Tender of Performance? (p. 190)
- What's Your Verdict? (pp. 186, 187, 190)
- Cultural Diversity in Law, *International* (p. 187, TE p. 190)
- In This Case (pp. 186, 188, 189, 190)
- A Question of Ethics (p. 186)
- Curriculum Connection, *Communication* (TE, p. 187)
- Curriculum Connection, *Communication/Social Studies* (TE, p. 189)
- Think Critically Through Visuals (TE, p. 188)

Apply
- Think About Legal Concepts 1-3 (p. 191)
- Think Critically About Evidence 4-6 (p. 191)

Assess
- Lesson 13-2 Quiz (Unit 2 Resource Book, p. 102)
- Reteach
  Have students create a spider map identifying five ways a contract may be discharged. Then have them add an example of each in additional spokes on the map.
- Enrich
  Have pairs of students write three examples of contracts discharged by impossibility because of destruction of subject matter, by the performance being declared illegal, or by death or disability of the party providing personal services under the terms of the contract.

Close
- Read and discuss *Prevent Legal Difficulties* on page 191.

Law for Business and Personal Use

Teacher: _____

Week of: _____

M   T   W   Th   F

Chapter 13 in Review
Pages 192-195

Teaching Resources
LAW LEARNING PACKAGE
- Chapter 13 Test (Unit 2 Resource Book, pp. 106-108)
- Interactive Business Law Study Guide Chapter 13
- WESTEST Chapter 13

Review
- Concepts in Brief 1-7 (p. 192)
- Your Legal Vocabulary 1-13 (p.192)
- Review Legal Concepts 14-17 (p. 193)
- Write About Legal Concepts 18-21 (p. 193)
- Think Critically About Evidence 22-26 (p. 193)
- Analyze Real Cases 27-30 (p. 194)

Apply
- Case for Legal Thinking (p. 195)
  - Practice Judging 1-2

Assess
- WESTEST Chapter 13
- Chapter 13 Test (Unit 2 Resource Book, pp. 106-108)

Law for Business and Personal Use

Teacher: _____
Week of: _____
       M   T   W   Th   F

Chapter 14   How Courts Enforce Contracts
pp. 196-209

Introduction
- Hot Debate (p. 196)

Chapter 14 Teaching Resources
LAW LEARNING PACKAGE
- Unit 2 Resource Book, pp. 112-121
- Transparencies 1, 2, 20
- Student Activities and Study Guide, pp. 87-94
- Lessons 14-1 and 14-2, Spanish Resources
- Interactive Business Law Study Guide Chapter 14
- WESTEST Chapter 14

Law for Business and Personal Use

Teacher: _____

Week of: _____

Lesson 14-1   Remedies for Breach of Contract
Pages 197-200

Goals
* Distinguish between minor and major breach
* Describe when the remedies of rescission and specific performance are available
* Define four types of damages and tell when they will be awarded by courts

Teaching Resources
LAW LEARNING PACKAGE
* Student Activities and Study Guide, pp. 87-90
* Transparencies 1, 20
* Unit 2 Resource Book, pp. 112-115
* Lesson 14-1 Spanish Resources

Focus
* Write "People keep their engagements when it is to the advantage of both not to break them." Discuss.

Teach
* Types of Breach and Remedies (pp. 197-199)
* Specific Performance (pp. 199-200)
* What's Your Verdict? (pp. 197, 199)
* In This Case (p. 198)
* Law and the Internet (p. 199)
* Curriculum Connection, *Math* (TE, p. 198)
* Think Critically Through Visuals (TE, p. 199)

Apply
* Think About Legal Concepts 1-3 (p. 200)
* Think Critically About Evidence 4-7 (p. 200)

Assess
* Lesson 14-1 Quiz (Unit 2 Resource Book, p. 112)
* Reteach
  Have students outline the lesson.
* Enrich
  Have students create a cartoon to visually describe one type of remedy for major breach of contract or to illustrate what it means to "place injured parties in the same financial position they would have been in if there had been no breach."

Close
* Review the lesson goals on page 197.

Law for Business and Personal Use   Teacher: _____
                                                        Week of: _____
                                                         M   T   W   Th   F

Lesson 14-2   Denial of Remedies for Breach of Contract
Pages 201-205

Goals
- Describe the election of remedies
- Describe the requirement to mitigate damages
- Explain how the statute of limitations and bankruptcy affect remedies for breach of contract

Teaching Resources
LAW LEARNING PACKAGE
- Student Activities and Study Guide, pp. 91-94
- Transparencies 1, 2
- Unit 2 Resource Book, pp. 116-119
- Lesson 14-2 Spanish Resources

Focus
- Write "Denial of Remedies for Breach of Contract" on the board. Have students use the letters in the title (only as many times as they actually appear) to write as many legal terms as they can.

Teach
- How Can Election of One Remedy Bar Use of Another Remedy? (p. 201)
- How Can Failure to Mitigate Damages Eliminate Remedies? (pp. 201-202)
- How Can Waiver Eliminate Remedies? (p. 202)
- How Can the Statute of Limitations Eliminate Remedies? (p. 203)
- How Can Bankruptcy Eliminate Remedies? (pp. 203-204)
- What's Your Verdict? (pp. 201, 202, 203)
- Cultural Diversity in Law, *International* (p. 204)
- In This Case (p. 203)
- A Question of Ethics (p. 202)
- Curriculum Connection, *Social Studies* (TE, p. 203)
- Think Critically Through Visuals (TE, p. 201, 202, 204)

Apply
- Think About Legal Concepts 1-6 (p. 204)
- Think Critically About Evidence 7-10 (p. 205)

Assess
- Lesson 14-2 Quiz (Unit 2 Resource Book, p. 116)
- Reteach
  Have pairs of students list two things they have learned about each of the following subjects: how election of one remedy can bar use of another remedy, mitigation of damages, waiver, statutes of limitations, and bankruptcy.
- Enrich
  Have groups of students investigate the specific statutes of limitations for oral and written contracts in their state. Then create a poster illustrating the most interesting or important point they discovered.

Close
- Assign a different point in *Prevent Legal Difficulties* on page 205 to a group of students. Have each group make a visual, oral, or dramatic presentation of their point to the class.

Law for Business and Personal Use   Teacher: _____
                                               Week of: _____
                                                        M   T   W   Th   F

Chapter 14 in Review
Pages 206-209

Teaching Resources
LAW LEARNING PACKAGE
- Chapter 14 Test (Unit 2 Resource Book, pp. 120-121)
- Interactive Business Law Study Guide Chapter 14
- WESTEST Chapter 14

Review
- Concepts in Brief 1-6 (p. 206)
- Your Legal Vocabulary 1-10 (p.206)
- Review Legal Concepts 11-14 (p. 207)
- Write About Legal Concepts 15-17 (p. 207)
- Think Critically About Evidence 18-22 (p. 207)
- Analyze Real Cases 23-28 (p. 208)

Apply
- Case for Legal Thinking (p. 209)
  - Practice Judging 1-3

Assess
- WESTEST Chapter 14
- Chapter 14 Test (Unit 2 Resource Book, pp. 120-121)

Unit 2   Fundamentals of Contracts (Chapters 7-14)
pp. 96-211
Wrap-Up
- Entrepreneurs and the Law (pp. 210-211)
  - Project 2 Fundamentals of Contracts

Law for Business and Personal Use

Teacher: _____

Week of: _____

| M | T | W | Th | F |

Unit 3   Law, Justice, and You   (Chapters 15-18)
pp. 212-279

Introduction
- In Practice Profile: Kathryn Redwine, Attorney (p. 213)

Chapter 15   Sales Contracts
pp. 214-229

Introduction
- Hot Debate (p. 214)

Chapter 15 Teaching Resources
LAW LEARNING PACKAGE
- Unit 3 Resource Book, pp. 5-18
- Transparencies 1, 2, 22
- Student Activities and Study Guide, pp. 95-102
- Lessons 15-1, 15-2, and 15-3 Spanish Resources
- Interactive Business Law Study Guide Chapter 15
- WESTEST Chapter 15

Law for Business and Personal Use

Teacher: _____

Week of: _____

M   T   W   Th   F

Lesson 15-1   Sales
Pages 215-218

Goals
- Define sale and explain how the UCC governs the sale of goods
- Identify unconscionable contracts and contracts of adhesion
- Distinguish between payment, delivery, and transfer of title of goods

Teaching Resources
LAW LEARNING PACKAGE
- Student Activities and Study Guide, pp. 95-96
- Transparency 1
- Unit 3 Resource Book, pp. 5-8
- Lesson 15-1 Spanish Resources

Focus
- Write "What is a sale?" on the board. Discuss and define *sale*.

Teach
- What is a Sale? (pp. 215-216)
- Must Delivery and Payment Be Made at the Same Time? (p. 216)
- Other Methods of Sales Contracting Under the UCC (p. 217)
- Unconscionable Sales Contracts (pp. 217-218)
- What's Your Verdict? (pp. 215, 216, 217)
- In This Case (p. 217)
- Think Critically Through Visuals (TE, pp. 216, 217)

Apply
- Think About Legal Concepts 1-5 (p. 218)
- Think Critically About Evidence 6-9 (p. 218)

Assess
- Lesson 15-1 Quiz (Unit 3 Resource Book, p. 5)
- Reteach
Write the vocabulary words on the board. Separate the class into two groups. The first person in the first group must define the first word on the list. If he or she misses, the first person in the other group tries. The team that gets it right scores and moves on to the next word until a team member misses. Once all words are defined, begin at the top of the word list again until all students have had a chance to participate.
- Enrich
Have students role-play various sales transactions, such as a bartering situation, a contract to sell, etc.

Close
- Have students write a short summary of this lesson.

Law for Business and Personal Use   Teacher: _____
                                                       Week of: _____
                                                                M   T   W   Th   F

Lesson 15-2   Ownership
Pages 219-221

Goals
- Discuss the benefits and burdens of ownership of property
- Compare the various methods of acquiring property
- Explain the unique role of merchants and why and how they are treated specially by the law

Teaching Resources
LAW LEARNING PACKAGE
- Student Activities and Study Guide, pp. 99-100
- Transparencies 1, 2, 22
- Unit 3 Resource Book, pp. 9-12
- Lesson 15-2 Spanish Resources

Focus
- Write "Do you have the right to do whatever you want with your property?" on the board. Discuss.
- Create lists on the board of items students say they own, what they like about ownership, and what they don't like about ownership.

Teach
- Results of Ownership (p. 219)
- Sales Compared with Other Transfers of Ownership and Possession (p. 220)
- What's Your Verdict? (pp. 219, 220)
- A Question of Ethics (p. 219)
- Curriculum Connection, *Social Studies* (TE, p. 220)

Apply
- Think About Legal Concepts 1-13 (p. 221)
- Think Critically About Evidence 14-17 (p. 221)

Assess
- Lesson 15-2 Quiz (Unit 3 Resource Book, p. 9)
- Reteach
Have students imagine they received a car as a gift. Have students create a comparison chart to identify the benefits and duties/burdens of owning this car.
- Enrich
  Have students create and role-play a feature news broadcast about the different transactions described in the chart on page 220. You may wish to videotape the broadcast and show it to another class.

Close
- Review questions in *What's Your Verdict?* on page 220.

Law for Business and Personal Use

Teacher: _____

Week of: _____

M   T   W   Th   F

Lesson 15-3   Special Rules for Sales Contracts
Pages 222-225

Goals
- Explain the need for the statute of frauds
- Discuss the instances in which the statute of frauds will be applied

Teaching Resources
LAW LEARNING PACKAGE
- Student Activities and Study Guide, pp. 101-102
- Transparency 1
- Unit 3 Resource Book, pp. 13-16
- Lesson 15-3 Spanish Resources

Focus
- Write "Why is the statute of frauds necessary?" on the board. Discuss.

Teach
- Statute of Frauds (p. 222)
- When Is a Signed Writing Not Required Under the Statute? (pp. 223-224)
- What's Your Verdict? (pp. 222, 223)
- Cultural Diversity in Law, *International* (p. 222; TE p. 223)
- In This Case (pp. 223, 224)
- Think Critically Through Visuals (TE, p. 225)

Apply
- Think About Legal Concepts 1-5 (p. 224)
- Think Critically About Evidence 6-8 (p. 224)

Assess
- Lesson 15-3 Quiz (Unit 3 Resource Book, p. 13)
- Reteach
  Have students work together to create and role-play scenarios about the statute of frauds.
- Enrich
  Have students work in groups to contact merchants in your community to find out about the merchant's sales policy. Have students prepare a written set of interview questions ahead of time.

Close
- Review questions in *What's Your Verdict?* on page 13.
- Read and discuss *Prevent Legal Difficulties* on page 225.

Law for Business and Personal Use

Teacher: _____
Week of: _____
              M   T   W   Th   F

Chapter 15 in Review
Pages 226-229

Teaching Resources
LAW LEARNING PACKAGE
- Chapter 15 Test (Unit 3 Resource Book, pp. 17-18)
- Interactive Business Law Study Guide Chapter 15
- WESTEST Chapter 15

Review
- Concepts in Brief 1-11 (p. 226)
- Your Legal Vocabulary 1-8 (p. 226)
- Review Legal Concepts 9-12 (p. 227)
- Write About Legal Concepts 13-15 (p. 227)
- Think Critically About Evidence 16-21 (p. 227)
- Analyze Real Cases 22-27 (p. 228)

Apply
- Case for Legal Thinking (p. 229)
  - Practice Judging 1-3

Assess
- WESTEST Chapter 15
- Chapter 15 Test (Unit 3 Resource Book, pp. 17-18)

Law for Business and Personal Use

Teacher: _____

Week of: _____

M	T	W	Th	F

Chapter 16   Ownership and Risk of Loss in Sales Transactions
pp. 230-243

Introduction

- Hot Debate (p. 230)

Chapter 16 Teaching Resources

LAW LEARNING PACKAGE

- Unit 3 Resource Book, pp. 25-34
- Transparencies 1, 2
- Student Activities and Study Guide, pp. 103-110
- Lessons 16-1 and 16-2 Spanish Resources
- Interactive Business Law Study Guide Chapter 16
- WESTEST Chapter 16

Law for Business and Personal Use

Teacher: _____

Week of: _____

M   T   W   Th   F

Lesson 16-1   The Power to Transfer Ownership
Pages 231-234

Goals
- Describe various types of goods
- Discuss who may transfer ownership of goods
- Explain what is required for transfer of ownership of goods
- Identify when the ownership of goods has transferred

Teaching Resources

LAW LEARNING PACKAGE
- Student Activities and Study Guide, pp. 103-106
- Transparencies 1, 2
- Unit 3 Resource Book, pp. 25-28
- Lesson 16-1 Spanish Resources

Focus
- Write "Who may transfer ownership of goods?" on the board. Discuss.

Teach
- Who May Transfer the Ownership of Goods? (pp. 231-232)
- Requirements for Transfer of Ownership (pp. 232-233)
- When Does Ownership Transfer? (pp. 233-234)
- What's Your Verdict? (pp. 231, 232, 233))
- Cultural Diversity in Law, *International* (p. 232)
- In This Case (pp. 231, 232)
- A Question of Ethics (p. 234)
- Think Critically Through Visuals (TE, p. 233)

Apply
- Think About Legal Concepts 1-5 (p. 234)
- Think Critically About Evidence 6-8 (p. 234)

Assess
- Lesson 16-1 Quiz (Unit 3 Resource Book, p. 25)

Reteach

   On the board write *existing goods, identified goods, future goods*, and *fungible goods*. Discuss and define each term.
- Enrich

   Assign each group of students a sales scenario, such as the sales of a custom-ordered computer system, a dozen cartons of CDs, or five horses from a herd of 20. Have each group write a sales memorandum, including evidence of existing, future, identified, or fungible goods as appropriate.

Close
- Review questions in *What's Your Verdict?* on pages 231 and 233.

Law for Business and Personal Use

Teacher: _____

Week of: _____

M	T	W	Th	F

Lesson 16-2   Risk of Loss and Insurable Interest
Pages 235-239

Goals
- Explain when the risk of loss from seller to buyer transfers in different situations
- Explain when insurable property interests transfer in different situations

Teaching Resources
LAW LEARNING PACKAGE
- Student Activities and Study Guide, pp. 107-110
- Transparency 1
- Unit 3 Resource Book, pp. 29-32
- Lesson 16-2 Spanish Resources

Focus
- Write the following on the board in a flow-chart sequence:
  - Seller ships goods by carrier
  - Goods held by bailee
  - Either party breaches after goods identified
  - Goods neither shipped by carrier nor held by bailee
- Explain and discuss the four possible alternatives.

Teach
- When Does Risk of Loss Transfer? (pp. 235-236)
- When Do Insurable Property Interests Transfer? (pp. 236-237)
- Transfer of Ownership and Risk of Loss in Specific Transactions (pp. 237-238)
- What's Your Verdict? (pp. 235, 236, 237)
- In This Case (pp. 235, 236, 238)
- Curriculum Connection, *Arts* (TE, p. 236)
- Curriculum Connection, *Economics* (TE, p. 237)
- Curriculum Connection, *Communication* (TE, p. 238)
- Think Critically Through Visuals (TE, p. 235)

Apply
- Think About Legal Concepts 1-6 (p. 238)
- Think Critically About Evidence 7-10 (p. 239)

Assess
- Lesson 16-2 Quiz (Unit 3 Resource Book, p. 29)
- Reteach
Have students work in pairs. One student is the buyer and the other student is the seller. Have students brainstorm ways to protect themselves in the following transactions: seller ships goods by carrier; goods held by a bailee; sales on credit; sale or return; and auction.
- Enrich
Have students work in groups to come up with five ideas that are relevant to their lives about transfer of ownership and risk of loss. Combine ideas and display in a classroom chart.

Close
- Read and discuss *Prevent Legal Difficulties* on page 239.
- Have the class outline this chapter. Discuss main points and write them on the board, then add details.

Law for Business and Personal Use

Teacher: _____
Week of: _____

      M   T   W   Th   F

Chapter 16 in Review
Pages 240-243

Teaching Resources
LAW LEARNING PACKAGE
- Chapter 16 Test (Unit 3 Resource Book, pp. 33-34)
- Interactive Business Law Study Guide Chapter 16
- WESTEST Chapter 16

Review
- Concepts in Brief 1-9 (p. 240)
- Your Legal Vocabulary 1-9 (p. 240)
- Review Legal Concepts 10-13 (p. 241)
- Write About Legal Concepts 14-16 (p. 241)
- Think Critically About Evidence 17-19 (p. 241)
- Analyze Real Cases 20-24 (p. 242)

Apply
- Case for Legal Thinking (p. 243)
  - Practice Judging 1-3

Assess
- WESTEST Chapter 16
- Chapter 16 Test (Unit 3 Resource Book, pp. 33-34)

Law for Business and Personal Use

Chapter 17   Consumer Protection
pp. 244-261

Introduction
- Hot Debate (p. 244)

Chapter 17 Teaching Resources
LAW LEARNING PACKAGE
- Unit 3 Resource Book, pp. 39-52
- Transparencies 1, 2, 23, 24
- Student Activities and Study Guide, pp. 111-120
- Lessons 17-1, 17-2, and 17-3 Spanish Resources
- Interactive Business Law Study Guide Chapter 17
- WESTEST Chapter 17

Law for Business and Personal Use   Teacher: _____
                                                     Week of: _____
                                                         M   T   W   Th   F

Lesson 17-1   Federal Protection
Pages 245-249

Goals
* Explain why and how the law focuses on protection of consumers
* Discuss the trade practices that are prohibited by consumer law

Teaching Resources
LAW LEARNING PACKAGE
* Student Activities and Study Guide, pp. 111-114
* Transparencies 1, 23
* Unit 3 Resource Book, pp. 29-42
* Lesson 17-1 Spanish Resources

Focus
* Write "Who is a consumer?" on the board. Discuss.
* Discuss what "caveat emptor" means.

Teach
* Why Does the Law Protect Consumers? (p. 245)
* Protection Against Substandard Goods (pp. 246-247)
* Protection Against Unfair Trade Practices (pp. 247-249)
* What's Your Verdict? (pp. 245, 246, 247)
* Law and the Internet (p. 248)
* Curriculum Connection, *Language Arts* (TE, pp. 246, 248)
* Curriculum Connection, *Art/Social Science* (TE, p. 247)
* Think Critically Through Visuals (TE, p. 246)

Apply
* Think About Legal Concepts 1-5 (p. 249)
* Think Critically About Evidence 6-8 (p. 249)

Assess
* Lesson 17-1 Quiz (Unit 3 Resource Book, p. 39)
* Reteach
Invite peer tutors to work with a partner to write a news feature about this chapter. Have partners present the newscast to the class.
* Enrich
Invite a consumer reporter from the local radio or television station to speak to the class about cases of unfair business practices and how consumers can protect themselves. Students should prepare a list of questions prior to the reporter's arrival.

Close
* Review questions in *What's Your Verdict?* on pages 245, 246, 247.

Law for Business and Personal Use

Teacher: _____

Week of: _____

M   T   W   Th   F

Lesson 17-2   State and Local Protection and Product Liability
Pages 250-252

Goals
- Discuss the contribution of local and state governments to consumer protection
- Define product liability
- Explain how strict liability law can protect consumers injured by defective products

Teaching Resources
LAW LEARNING PACKAGE
- Student Activities and Study Guide, pp. 115-116
- Transparencies 1, 24
- Unit 3 Resource Book, pp. 43-46
- Lesson 17-2 Spanish Resources

Focus
- Write "What do you know about state and local government protection?" on the board. Discuss and make a list of students' answers.

Teach
- State and Local Government Protection (pp. 250-251)
- What Is Product Liability? (pp. 251-252)
- What's Your Verdict? (pp. 250-251)
- Cultural Diversity in Law, *Japan* (p. 251)
- FYI (p. 250)
- Think Critically Through Visuals (TE, p. 251)

Apply
- Think About Legal Concepts 1-4 (p. 252)
- Think Critically About Evidence 5-7 (p. 252)

Assess
- Lesson 17-2 Quiz (Unit 3 Resource Book, p. 43)
- Reteach
Invite someone from your community's public buildings inspection office to speak to the class. Ask this person to bring copies of local building codes and have students identify safety laws for public buildings.
- Enrich
Invite representatives from the Better Business Bureau, your chamber of commerce, and the state attorney's office to speak as a panel to the class about consumer protection. Students should prepare a list of questions before the panel speaks.

Close
- Have the class summarize how the various agencies and laws protect consumers.

Law for Business and Personal Use

Teacher: _____

Week of: _____

M   T   W   Th   F

Lesson 17-3   Warranties
Pages 253-257

Goals
- Distinguish between implied and express warranties and explain the protection they provide
- Explain the warranty of merchantability and how it may be limited or excluded
- Differentiate between a full and a limited warranty

Teaching Resources
LAW LEARNING PACKAGE
- Student Activities and Study Guide, pp. 117-120
- Transparencies 1, 2
- Unit 3 Resource Book, pp. 47-50
- Lesson 17-3 Spanish Resources

Focus
- Write "What is a warranty?" on the board. Make lists of what students know and what they need to learn about.

Teach
- Express and Implied Warranties (pp. 253-254)
- Implied Warranties (pp. 254-255)
- Additional Information About Warranties (pp. 255-256)
- What's Your Verdict? (pp. 253, 254, 255)
- In This Case (p. 254, 256)
- A Question of Ethics (p. 254)
- Curriculum Connection, *Language Arts* (TE, p. 254)
- Curriculum Connection, *Economics* (TE, p. 255)
- Think Critically Through Visuals (TE, p. 256)

Apply
- Think About Legal Concepts 1-4 (p. 257)
- Think Critically About Evidence 5-7 (p. 257)

Assess
- Lesson 17-3 Quiz (Unit 3 Resource Book, p. 47)
- Reteach

Have students work in groups to discuss one type of warranties covered in this lesson. Each group is to provide the class with a summary of a consumer's rights under the warranty and give an example. Be sure all warranties are covered, even if some groups must cover more than one type of warranty.

- Enrich

Have students debate the following: *All warranties should be express.* One group should argue warranties should be express. The other group should argue that an implied warranty is enough.

Close
- Review the vocabulary words by writing each on the board. For each term, have one student define it and another student use it correctly in a sentence.

Law for Business and Personal Use

Chapter 17 in Review
Pages 258-261

Teaching Resources
LAW LEARNING PACKAGE
*   Chapter 17 Test (Unit 3 Resource Book, pp. 51-52)
*   Interactive Business Law Study Guide Chapter 17
*   WESTEST Chapter 17

Review
*   Concepts in Brief 1-6 (p. 258)
*   Your Legal Vocabulary 1-15 (p. 258)
*   Review Legal Concepts 16-21 (p. 259)
*   Write About Legal Concepts 22-24 (p. 259)
*   Think Critically About Evidence 25-30 (p. 259)
*   Analyze Real Cases 31-35 (p. 260)

Apply
*   Case for Legal Thinking (p. 261)
    *   Practice Judging 1-3

Assess
*   WESTEST Chapter 17
*   Chapter 17 Test (Unit 3 Resource Book, pp. 51-52)

Law for Business and Personal Use

Chapter 18 Legal Considerations in Marriage and Divorce
pp. 262-277

Introduction
• Hot Debate (p. 262)

Chapter 18 Teaching Resources
LAW LEARNING PACKAGE
• Unit 3 Resource Book, pp. 57-66
• Transparencies 1, 2, 25
• Student Activities and Study Guide, pp. 121-124
• Lessons 18-1 and 18-2 Spanish Resources
• Interactive Business Law Study Guide Chapter 18
• WESTEST Chapter 18

Law for Business and Personal Use

Teacher: _____

Week of: _____

| M | T | W | Th | F |

Lesson 18-1   Legal Aspects of Marriage
Pages 263-268

Goals
- Discuss how the law affects premarital and marital relationships
- Explain the uses of prenuptial agreements
- Name the rights and duties of husbands and wives

Teaching Resources
LAW LEARNING PACKAGE
- Student Activities and Study Guide, pp. 121-122
- Transparencies 1, 25
- Unit 3 Resource Book, pp. 57-60
- Lesson 18-1 Spanish Resources

Focus
- Write "Do you plan on getting married?" on the board.
- On the board make lists of students' ideas about "a dream marriage" and "a realistic marriage." Have students copy the lists for use in the reteaching activity at the end of the lesson.

Teach
- Premarital Relationships (p. 263)
- The Marital Contract (pp. 263-264)
- How Do You Get Married? (p. 264)
- Duties and Rights of Wives and Husbands (pp. 265-267)
- What's Your Verdict? (pp. 263, 264, 265)
- Cultural Diversity in Law, *Muslim Culture* (p. 263)
- Cultural Diversity in Law, *Massachusetts & Tennessee* (p. 265)
- Curriculum Connection, *Social Science/Language Arts* (TE, pp. 266, 267)
- Think Critically Through Visuals (TE, pp. 264, 265)

Apply
- Think About Legal Concepts 1-9 (p. 268)
- Think Critically About Evidence 10-15 (p. 268)

Assess
- Lesson 18-1 Quiz (Unit 3 Resource Book, p. 51)
- Reteach
Have students look at the lists for "a dream marriage" and "a realistic marriage" that they copied at the beginning of the lesson. Ask students to use a different colored pen and make appropriate changes to their lists using the information from this lesson.
- Enrich
Have a marriage counselor speak to the class about typical problems married couples encounter. Also ask the counselor to provide tips on improving relationships with all people. The tips should be appropriate for the students.

Close
- Review this lesson by having student pairs write a summary of the chapter.

Law for Business and Personal Use   Teacher: _____
                                                       Week of: _____
                                                       M   T   W   Th   F

Lesson 18-2   Legal Aspects of Divorce
Pages 269-273

Goals
- Discuss ways other than divorce by which marriages can end
- Identify grounds for a traditional and a no-fault divorce
- Name topics usually covered in a separation agreement

Teaching Resources
LAW LEARNING PACKAGE
- Student Activities and Study Guide, pp. 123-124
- Transparencies 1, 2
- Unit 3 Resource Book, pp. 61-64
- Lesson 18-2 Spanish Resources

Focus
- Write "Why do some marriages end in divorce?" on the board. Discuss.

Teach
- Ending Marriages Legally (pp. 269-270)
- Marriage Ended by Divorce (pp. 270-272)
- What's Your Verdict? (pp. 269, 270)
- Cultural Diversity in Law, *Louisiana* (p. 271)
- A Question of Ethics (p. 272)
- Law in the Media (p. 269)
- Law and the Internet (p. 270)
- Curriculum Connection, *Language Arts* (TE, pp. 270, 271)
- Think Critically Through Visuals (TE, pp. 270, 272)

Apply
- Think About Legal Concepts 1-10 (p. 272)
- Think Critically About Evidence 11-17 (p. 273)

Assess
- Lesson 18-2 Quiz (Unit 3 Resource Book, p. 61)
- Reteach
Invite a divorce attorney to speak about the steps taken in a divorce in your state. Have students prepare
   questions before the attorney speaks.
- Enrich
   Have students interview someone from either another country or another generation to learn about
   divorce customs.

Close
- Write vocabulary words from the lesson on the boards. Call on students to define each word and to
   use each word in a sentence.
- Read and discuss *Prevent Legal Difficulties* on page 273.

Law for Business and Personal Use

Chapter 18 in Review
Pages 274-277

Teaching Resources

LAW LEARNING PACKAGE
- Chapter 18 Test (Unit 3 Resource Book, pp. 65-66)
- Interactive Business Law Study Guide Chapter 18
- WESTEST Chapter 18

Review
- Concepts in Brief 1-6 (p. 274)
- Your Legal Vocabulary 1-15 (p. 274)
- Review Legal Concepts 16-19 (p. 275)
- Write About Legal Concepts 20-22 (p. 275)
- Think Critically About Evidence 23-27 (p. 275)
- Analyze Real Cases 28-32 (p. 276)

Apply
- Case for Legal Thinking (p. 277)
  - Practice Judging 1-3

Assess
- WESTEST Chapter 18
- Chapter 18 Test (Unit 3 Resource Book, pp. 65-66)

Unit 3   Sales and Other Contractual Situations   (Chapters 15-18)
pp. 212-279

Wrap-Up
- Entrepreneurs and the Law (pp. 278-279)
  - Project 3 Sales and Other Contractual Situations
    Think Critically Through Visuals (TE, p. 279)

Law for Business and Personal Use   Teacher: _____

                                                             Week of: _____
                                                             M   T   W   Th   F

Unit 4   Property (Chapters 19-24)
pp. 280-375

Introduction

- In Practice Profile: Warren Zaretsky, Media Producer (p. 281)

Chapter 19   Property
pp. 282-297

Introduction

- Hot Debate (p. 282)

Chapter 19 Teaching Resources

LAW LEARNING PACKAGE

- Unit 4 Resource Book, pp. 5-16
- Transparencies 1, 2, 27, 28
- Student Activities and Study Guide, pp. 125-132
- Lessons 19-1, 19-2, and 19-3 Spanish Resources
- Interactive Business Law Study Guide Chapter 19
- WESTEST Chapter 19

Law for Business and Personal Use

Teacher: _____
Week of: _____

| M | T | W | Th | F |

Lesson 19-1   Classes of Property
Pages 283-286

Goals
*   Distinguish between real, tangible personal, and intangible personal property
*   Determine what body of law governs various transactions for the purchase of goods and/or services
*   Discuss the types of intellectual property

Teaching Resources
LAW LEARNING PACKAGE
*   Student Activities and Study Guide, pp. 125-128
*   Transparencies 1, 27
*   Unit 4 Resource Book, pp. 5-8
*   Lesson 19-1 Spanish Resources

Focus
*   Write "What do you think property is?" on the board. Discuss.

Teach
*   What Is Property? (p. 283)
*   Classifications of Property (pp. 283-285)
*   What's Your Verdict? (p. 283)
*   Cultural Diversity in Law, *Trademark Protection* (p. 285)
*   In This Case (p. 284)
*   Law and the Internet (p. 284)
*   Curriculum Connection, *Language Arts* (TE, p. 284)

Apply
*   Think About Legal Concepts 1-9 (p. 286)
*   Think Critically About Evidence 10-13 (p. 286)

Assess
*   Lesson 19-1 Quiz (Unit 4 Resource Book, p. 5)
*   Reteach
Secure a large sheet of butcher paper to a classroom wall. Label it *Advice about Real and Personal Property*. Invite students to use different colored markers, paints, or crayons to write and draw a graffiti wall about the information in this lesson.
*   Enrich
Have students work in groups. Have each group create a collage that displays different forms of real and personal property.

Close
*   Ask students to name examples of real and personal property, including intellectual property and to name how each is protected.

Law for Business and Personal Use

Teacher: _____

Week of: _____

M   T   W   Th   F

Lesson 19-2   Acquiring Property
Pages 287-290

Goals
- Discuss seven ways of acquiring property
- Distinguish between mislaid and lost property
- Identify some of the legal limitations on the use of property

Teaching Resources

LAW LEARNING PACKAGE
- Student Activities and Study Guide, pp. 129-130
- Transparencies 1, 2
- Unit 4 Resource Book, pp. 9-12
- Lesson 19-2 Spanish Resources

Focus
- Write "How have you acquired property?" on the board. Discuss.

Teach
- How Is Property Acquired? (pp. 287-289)
- Limitations on Ownership (p. 289)
- What's Your Verdict? (pp. 287, 289)
- Cultural Diversity in Law, *Medieval England* (p. 289)
- In This Case (p. 287)
- A Question of Ethics (p. 288)
- Law and the Internet (p. 288)
- Think Critically Through Visuals (TE, p. 288)

Apply
- Think About Legal Concepts 1-8 (p. 290)
- Think Critically About Evidence 9-14 (p. 290)

Assess
- Lesson 19-2 Quiz (Unit 4 Resource Book, p. 9)
- Reteach

Have students complete a personal property inventory. Have them list at least 10 items and name the method by which ownership came to them.
- Enrich

Have students write a fictional story about how they became the owner of a piece of real or personal property.

Close
- Have students list the different ways to obtain property on the board. Then have students give facts about this type of ownership. Every time a student gives a correct example, he or she gets a point. The student with the most points wins a prize.

Law for Business and Personal Use

Teacher: _____
Week of: _____
        M   T   W   Th   F

Lesson 19-3   Forms of Ownership
Pages 291-293

Goals
- Distinguish between the two basic ways to own property
- Describe the features of each form of co-ownership

Teaching Resources
LAW LEARNING PACKAGE
- Student Activities and Study Guide, pp. 131-132
- Transparencies 1, 2, 28
- Unit 4 Resource Book, pp. 13-16
- Lesson 19-3 Spanish Resources

Focus
- Write "What do I need to know about owning property with someone?" Discuss.

Teach
- Property Ownership (pp. 291-292)
- What's Your Verdict? (p. 291)
- In This Case (p. 292)
- A Question of Ethics (p. 291)
- Think Critically Through Visuals (TE, p. 292)

Apply
- Think About Legal Concepts 1-7 (p. 293)
- Think Critically About Evidence 8-11 (p. 293)

Assess
- Lesson 19-3 Quiz (Unit 4 Resource Book, p. 13)
- Reteach
Separate students into four groups. On index cards write one of the following: *joint tenancy, tenancy in common, tenancy by the entireties,* and *community property.* Give each group an index card. Using art materials, students are to create a chart that explains their type of ownership.
- Enrich
Tell students they are starting a computer graphic design business with a financial backer. The partnership will be by tenancy in partnership. Have students write an agreement for co-ownership of the equipment and the clients. Their agreement should cover what would happen if they sold or dissolved the business or if one of them should die.

Close
- Read and discuss *Prevent Legal Difficulties* on page 293.

Law for Business and Personal Use

Teacher: _____
Week of: _____

| M | T | W | Th | F |

Chapter 19 in Review
Pages 294-297

Teaching Resources
LAW LEARNING PACKAGE
- Chapter 19 Test (Unit 4 Resource Book, pp. 17-18)
- Interactive Business Law Study Guide Chapter 19
- WESTEST Chapter 19

Review
- Concepts in Brief 1-6 (p. 294)
- Your Legal Vocabulary 1-16 (p. 294)
- Review Legal Concepts 17-20 (p. 295)
- Write About Legal Concepts 21-24 (p. 295)
- Think Critically About Evidence 25-28 (p. 295)
- Analyze Real Cases 29-36 (p. 296)

Apply
- Case for Legal Thinking (p. 297)
  - Practice Judging 1-3

Assess
- WESTEST Chapter 19
- Chapter 19 Test (Unit 4 Resource Book, pp. 17-18)

Law for Business and Personal Use

Teacher: _____
Week of: _____
      M   T   W   Th   F

Chapter 20   Bailments
pp. 298-311

Introduction
- Hot Debate (p. 298)

Chapter 20 Teaching Resources
LAW LEARNING PACKAGE
- Unit 4 Resource Book, pp. 23-36
- Transparencies 1, 2
- Student Activities and Study Guide, pp. 133-140
- Lessons 20-1, 20-2, and 20-3 Spanish Resources
- Interactive Business Law Study Guide Chapter 20
- WESTEST Chapter 20

Law for Business and Personal Use

Teacher: _____

Week of: _____

M   T   W   Th   F

Lesson 20-1   Bailment Relations
Pages 299-301

Goals
- Identify the legal names for parties to bailments
- Determine when a bailment arises and ends

Teaching Resources
LAW LEARNING PACKAGE
- Student Activities and Study Guide, pp. 133-134
- Transparencies 1, 2
- Unit 4 Resource Book, pp. 23-26
- Lesson 20-1 Spanish Resources

Focus
- Write "What bailments have you been involved in?" on the board. Discuss.

Teach
- How Is a Bailment Created? (pp. 299-300)
- How Does a Bailment End? (p. 300)
- What's Your Verdict? (pp. 299, 300)
- A Question of Ethics (p. 299)

Apply
- Think About Legal Concepts 1-5 (p. 300)
- Think Critically About Evidence 6-9 (p. 300)

Assess
- Lesson 20-1 Quiz (Unit 4 Resource Book, p. 23)
- Reteach

Have each student use colored pencils or markers to create a spider map to identify the four characteristics that must be present for bailment to exist. Then have student groups brainstorm examples of bailments and create a map to depict the bailment attributes of each example.
- Enrich

Have students work in groups to decide whether a bailment exists in situations, such as: leaving a car in a park-and-lock lot, leaving shoes at a shoe repair shop, finding a classmate's purse at a basketball game, or borrowing a sweater from a friend.

Close
- Review the vocabulary words by writing each word on the board. Have students write a sentence for each word to demonstrate knowledge of its meaning.

Law for Business and Personal Use

Teacher: _____

Week of: _____

M   T   W   Th   F

Lesson 20-2   Duties in Bailments
Pages 301-304

Goals
- Identify types of bailments
- Identify the duties of bailees and bailors
- Describe how to modify a bailee's duty of care

Teaching Resources
LAW LEARNING PACKAGE
- Student Activities and Study Guide, pp. 135-138
- Transparency 1
- Unit 4 Resource Book, pp. 27-30
- Lesson 20-2 Spanish Resources

Focus
- Create the following graphic organizer on the board:

4 Characteristics of Bailments

personal property   transfer of temporary possession
transfer of temporary control   both parties intend return of goods

Levels of Care

extraordinary care   ordinary care   minimal care

Have students fill in the organizer with key words as they study the lesson.

Teach
- Bailee's Duty of Care (pp. 301-303)
- Bailor's Duty of Care Concerning Property Condition (p. 303)
- What Is the Bailee's Duty to Return the Goods? (pp. 303-304)
- What's Your Verdict? (p. 301, 303)
- Cultural Diversity in Law, *International* (p. 302, TE p. 303)
- In This Case (pp. 302, 303)
- FYI (p. 302)
- Think Critically Through Visuals (TE, p. 302)

Apply
- Think About Legal Concepts 1-6 (p. 304)
- Think Critically About Evidence 7-12 (p. 304)

Assess
- Lesson 20-2 Quiz (Unit 4 Resource Book, p. 27)
- Reteach
Have students work in groups on the graphic organizer started in the *Focus* section of the lesson. They
   may wish to create one large, colorful organizer.
- Enrich
   Have students work in groups to write a scenario that involves a situation where a bailee's lien is
   required or the goods are returned. Have students act out their scenarios.

Close
- Have students work with a partner and role-play each of the three ways to modify the nature of a
   bailee's duty of care.

Law for Business and Personal Use

Teacher: _____
Week of: _____

M   T   W   Th   F

Lesson 20-3   Common Bailments
Pages 305-307

Goals
* List the most common types of bailments
* Describe the legal features of the most common types of bailments

Teaching Resources
LAW LEARNING PACKAGE
* Student Activities and Study Guide, pp. 139-140
* Transparency 1
* Unit 4 Resource Book, pp. 31-34
* Lesson 20-3 Spanish Resources

Focus
* Write "What items might be shipped by common carrier?" on the board. Discuss.

Teach
* Bailment for Transport (p. 305)
* Bailment for Hire (p. 305)
* Bailment for Services (pp. 305-306)
* Bailment for Sale (p. 306)
* What's Your Verdict? (pp. 305, 306)
* Think Critically Through Visuals (TE, p. 306)

Apply
* Think About Legal Concepts 1-5 (p. 306)
* Think Critically About Evidence 6-10 (p. 307)

Assess
* Lesson 20-3 Quiz (Unit 4 Resource Book, p. 31)
* Reteach
Have each student choose one section from this lesson and write a summary of their learning. Share the
    results with the class.
* Enrich
    Have students create a poem or song that demonstrates their learning in this lesson. Have students
    share their results with the class.

Close
* Read and discuss *Prevent Legal Difficulties* on page 307.
* Have each student outline the lesson.

Law for Business and Personal Use

Teacher: _____

Week of: _____

M   T   W   Th   F

Chapter 20 in Review
Pages 308-311

Teaching Resources
LAW LEARNING PACKAGE
- Chapter 20 Test (Unit 4 Resource Book, pp. 35-36)
- Interactive Business Law Study Guide Chapter 20
- WESTEST Chapter 20

Review
- Concepts in Brief 1-7 (p. 308)
- Your Legal Vocabulary 1-12 (p. 308)
- Review Legal Concepts 13-16 (p. 309)
- Write About Legal Concepts 17-18 (p. 309)
- Think Critically About Evidence 19-22 (p. 309)
- Analyze Real Cases 23-31 (p. 310)

Apply
- Case for Legal Thinking (p. 311)
  - Practice Judging 1-3

Assess
- WESTEST Chapter 20
- Chapter 20 Test (Unit 4 Resource Book, pp. 35-36)

Law for Business and Personal Use

Chapter 21   Real Property
pp. 312-327

Introduction
- Hot Debate (p. 312)

Chapter 21 Teaching Resources
LAW LEARNING PACKAGE
- Unit 4 Resource Book, pp. 41-54
- Transparencies 1, 2
- Student Activities and Study Guide, pp. 41-52
- Lessons 21-1, 21-2, and 21-3 Spanish Resources
- Interactive Business Law Study Guide Chapter 21
- WESTEST Chapter 21

Law for Business and Personal Use

Teacher: _____

Week of: _____

       M   T   W   Th   F

Lesson 21-1   What Is Real Property?
Pages 313-315

Goals
- Identify the physical and legal elements of real property
- Describe the major tests used to distinguish real and personal property
- Classify items as real or personal

Teaching Resources
LAW LEARNING PACKAGE
- Student Activities and Study Guide, pp. 141-144
- Transparency 1
- Unit 4 Resource Book, pp. 41-44
- Lesson 21-1 Spanish Resources

Focus
- Write "What do I need to know before I buy real property?" on the board. Discuss and record student answers on the board.

Teach
- Real Property Rights (p. 313)
- Real vs. Personal Property (pp. 314-315)
- What's Your Verdict? (pp. 313, 314)
- In This Case (p. 313)
- Think Critically Through Visuals (TE, p. 314)

Apply
- Think About Legal Concepts 1-6 (p. 315)
- Think Critically About Evidence 7-10 (p. 315)

Assess
- Lesson 21-1 Quiz (Unit 4 Resource Book, p. 41)
- Reteach

Have students make a wall collage entitled *Real and Personal Property*.
- Enrich

   Have students create a three-column charts with headings of: *Real Property, Personal Property,* and *Fixtures.* Students are to work with an adult family member to make a list of 10 items that fit into either real or personal property. Then have students put a check mark in the Fixtures column when appropriate.

Close
- Draw a plot of land, including such items as a house, tent, mobile home, trees, garden, the space below the surface, and the airspace above. Ask students to identify each item as either real or personal property.

Law for Business and Personal Use   Teacher: _____
                                             Week of: _____
                                                      M   T   W   Th   F

Lesson 21-2   Nature and Transfer of Ownership
Pages 316-319

Goals
- Describe the major estates in land
- Identify the legal names of parties involved in deeding realty
- Describe the processes for transferring ownership of land

Teaching Resources
LAW LEARNING PACKAGE
- Student Activities and Study Guide, pp. 145-148
- Transparencies 1, 2
- Unit 4 Resource Book, pp. 45-48
- Lesson 21-2 Spanish Resources

Focus
- Write "If you rent an apartment, who owns it?" on the board. Discuss.

Teach
- Major Estates in Land (pp. 316-317)
- Transfer of Ownership (pp. 317-318)
- What's Your Verdict? (p. 316, 317)
- Cultural Diversity in Law, *Honduras* (p. 316)
- A Question of Ethics (p. 318)
- Think Critically Through Visuals (TE, pp. 317, 318)

Apply
- Think About Legal Concepts 1-9 (p. 319)
- Think Critically About Evidence 10-14 (p. 319)

Assess
- Lesson 21-2 Quiz (Unit 4 Resource Book, p. 45)
- Reteach
Set up a panel of students. Have other students ask questions from the material within the lesson.
- Enrich
  Have students choose a panel of real estate agents to speak to the class. If possible, include specialists in rental property, in single-family houses, and in commercial real estate.

Close
- Have peer tutors work with students in pairs to make a list of vocabulary words and quiz each other on their meanings.

Law for Business and Personal Use

Teacher: _____

Week of: _____

M   T   W   Th   F

Lesson 21-3   Others' Rights in Your Land
Pages 320-323

Goals
* Describe and distinguish licenses and easements
* Describe when a restrictive covenant binds buyers
* Distinguish between valid and invalid zoning
* Describe the duties owners owe to persons injured on their realty

Teaching Resources
LAW LEARNING PACKAGE
* Student Activities and Study Guide, pp. 149-152
* Transparency 1
* Unit 4 Resource Book, pp. 49-52
* Lesson 21-3 Spanish Resources

Focus
* Write "What rights do other people have in your real property?" on the board. Discuss and record student answers on the board.

Teach
* Licenses and Easements (pp. 320-321)
* Restrictive Covenants and Zoning Ordinances (p. 321)
* Liens Filed Against Real Property (p. 322)
* Duties Owed to Those Entering Your Land (p. 322)
* What's Your Verdict? (pp. 320, 321, 322)
* Curriculum Connection, *Economics* (TE, p. 321)
* Curriculum Connection, *Government* (TE, p. 322)
* Think Critically Through Visuals (TE, p. 321)

Apply
* Think About Legal Concepts 1-4 (p. 323)
* Think Critically About Evidence 5-7 (p. 323)

Assess
* Lesson 21-3 Quiz (Unit 4 Resource Book, p. 49)
* Reteach
Invite a zoning officer to the classroom to speak about different zoning restrictions in your community, what they mean, and how a landowner can work to change them.
* Enrich
Invite a local insurance broker to discuss the cost of insurance to cover a homeowner and also a business.

Close
* Read and discuss *Prevent Legal Difficulties* on page 323.
* Review this chapter by having students take turns writing a summary on the board. Each student should contribute something.

Law for Business and Personal Use

Teacher: _____
Week of: _____
     M   T   W   Th   F

Chapter 21 in Review
Pages 324-327

Teaching Resources
LAW LEARNING PACKAGE
- Chapter 21 Test (Unit 4 Resource Book, pp. 53-54)
- Interactive Business Law Study Guide Chapter 21
- WESTEST Chapter 21

Review
- Concepts in Brief 1-8 (p. 324)
- Your Legal Vocabulary 1-11 (p. 324)
- Review Legal Concepts 12-15 (p. 325)
- Write About Legal Concepts 16-19 (p. 325)
- Think Critically About Evidence 20-25 (p. 325)
- Analyze Real Cases 26-31 (p. 326)

Apply
- Case for Legal Thinking (p. 327)
  - Practice Judging 1-2

Assess
- WESTEST Chapter 21
- Chapter 21 Test (Unit 4 Resource Book, pp. 53-54)

Law for Business and Personal Use

Teacher: _____

Week of: _____

          M   T   W   Th   F

Chapter 22   Renting Realty
pp. 328-341

Introduction

- Hot Debate (p. 328)

Chapter 22 Teaching Resources

LAW LEARNING PACKAGE

- Unit 4 Resource Book, pp. 59-72
- Transparencies 1, 2
- Student Activities and Study Guide, pp. 153-158
- Lessons 22-1, 22-2, and 22-3 Spanish Resources
- Interactive Business Law Study Guide Chapter 22
- WESTEST Chapter 22

Law for Business and Personal Use

Teacher: _____

Week of: _____

M   T   W   Th   F

Lesson 22-1   Types of Leases
Pages 329-331

Goals
- Describe the legal characteristics of a lease
- Identify the parties to a lease
- Describe the various leasehold estates

Teaching Resources
LAW LEARNING PACKAGE
- Student Activities and Study Guide, pp. 153-154
- Transparencies 1, 2
- Unit 4 Resource Book, pp. 59-62
- Lesson 22-1 Spanish Resources

Focus
- Create two charts of the board. Label one *Tenant* and the other *Landlord*. Under both titles, write *rights* and *duties*. Have various students write an entry under each category.

Teach
- What Is a Lease? (p. 329)
- Types of Leasehold Estates (pp. 329-330)
- What's Your Verdict? (p. 329)
- In This Case (pp. 329, 330)
- A Question of Ethics (p. 331)
- FYI (p. 331)
- Think Critically Through Visuals (TE, p. 330)

Apply
- Think About Legal Concepts 1-7 (p. 331)
- Think Critically About Evidence 8-10 (p. 331)

Assess
- Lesson 22-1 Quiz (Unit 4 Resource Book, p. 59)
- Reteach
Have pairs of students use colorful markers to draw a flowchart that shows the exchange of rights and considerations in a landlord/tenant relationship.
- Enrich
Have pairs of students role-play the tenant-landlord relationship.

Close
- Review questions in *What's Your Verdict?* on page 329.

Law for Business and Personal Use

Teacher: _____

Week of: _____

M   T   W   Th   F

Lesson 22-2   Tenant's Rights and Duties
Pages 332-334

Goals
- Explain the tenant's right to use the property
- Tell how a lease can be transferred
- Explain the duty to pay rent

Teaching Resources

LAW LEARNING PACKAGE
- Student Activities and Study Guide, pp. 155-156
- Transparency 1
- Unit 4 Resource Book, pp. 63-66
- Lesson 22-2 Spanish Resources

Focus
- Write "What rights do tenants have?" on the board. Have students make a list of tenant's rights on the board.

Teach
- Tenants' Rights (pp. 332-333)
- Tenants' Duties (p. 333)
- What's Your Verdict? (pp. 332, 333)
- Cultural Diversity in Law, *Mexico* (p. 332, TE p. 333)
- In This Case (p. 332)

Apply
- Think About Legal Concepts 1-7 (p. 334)
- Think Critically About Evidence 8-12 (p. 334)

Assess
- Lesson 22-2 Quiz (Unit 4 Resource Book, p. 63)
- Reteach

Have students bring newspaper ads for apartment and house rentals. Then have pairs of students role-play being the tenant and landlord with the tenant telephoning the landlord and asking questions about the property, including legal and personal questions.
- Enrich

Have students role-play the rights and duties of tenants for various scenarios, such as the landlord wants to evict the tenant because of non-payment of rent; the tenant is claiming a construction eviction and refusing to pay rent.

Close
- Have students turn the charts they make on the rights and duties of tenants into a graphic organizer.

Law for Business and Personal Use

Teacher: _____

Week of: _____

M   T   W   Th   F

Lesson 22-3   Landlord's Rights and Duties
Pages 335-337

Goals
- Describe the lessor's rights when rent is not paid and the lessor's duties to maintain the premises
- Tell when the lessor is liable for injuries on the property
- Describe the lessor's duties under the Fair Housing Act

Teaching Resources
LAW LEARNING PACKAGE
- Student Activities and Study Guide, pp. 157-158
- Transparency 1
- Unit 4 Resource Book, pp. 67-70
- Lesson 22-3 Spanish Resources

Focus
- Write "What are the landlord's rights and duties?" on the board. Have students make a list of rights and duties on the board.

Teach
- Landlords' Rights and Duties (pp. 335-336)
- What's Your Verdict? (p. 335)
- Law and the Internet (p. 336)
- Think Critically Through Visuals (TE, p. 336)

Apply
- Think About Legal Concepts 1-5 (p. 337)
- Think Critically About Evidence 6-7 (p. 337)

Assess
- Lesson 22-3 Quiz (Unit 4 Resource Book, p. 67)
- Reteach

Have students write a lease from the landlord's perspective that includes all the landlord's duties and
responsibilities. Also include in the lease what is expected of the tenant.
- Enrich

Invite a representative from a tenant's association and a landlord to sit on a panel and explain tenant's
and landlord's duties and responsibilities.

Close
- Read and discuss *Prevent Legal Difficulties* on page 337.
- Review this lesson by writing vocabulary words on the board. Have various students define the words
and other students contribute to a short summary of the lesson using each word.

Law for Business and Personal Use

Teacher: _____

Week of: _____

M   T   W   Th   F

Chapter 22 in Review
Pages 338-341

Teaching Resources
LAW LEARNING PACKAGE
- Chapter 22 Test (Unit 4 Resource Book, pp. 71-72)
- Interactive Business Law Study Guide Chapter 22
- WESTEST Chapter 22

Review
- Concepts in Brief 1-7 (p. 338)
- Your Legal Vocabulary 1-12 (p. 338)
- Review Legal Concepts 13-16 (p. 339)
- Write About Legal Concepts 17-20 (p. 339)
- Think Critically About Evidence 21-25 (p. 339)
- Analyze Real Cases 26-33 (p. 340)

Apply
- Case for Legal Thinking (p. 341)
  - Practice Judging 1-2

Assess
- WESTEST Chapter 22
- Chapter 22 Test (Unit 4 Resource Book, pp. 71-72)

Law for Business and Personal Use

Teacher: _____

Week of: _____

| | M | T | W | Th | F |

Chapter 23   Insuring Your Future
pp. 342-359

Introduction
- Hot Debate (p. 342)

Chapter 23 Teaching Resources

LAW LEARNING PACKAGE
- Unit 4 Resource Book, pp. 78-90
- Transparencies 1, 2, 29
- Student Activities and Study Guide, pp. 159-168
- Lessons 23-1, 23-2, and 23-3 Spanish Resources
- Interactive Business Law Study Guide Chapter 23
- WESTEST Chapter 23

Law for Business and Personal Use

Teacher: _____

Week of: _____

M   T   W   Th   F

Lesson 23-1   Insurance and How It Works
Pages 343-346

Goals
- Discuss the common types of insurance
- Identify when an insurable interest is present

Teaching Resources
LAW LEARNING PACKAGE
- Student Activities and Study Guide, pp. 159-162
- Transparencies 1, 29
- Unit 4 Resource Book, pp. 78-80
- Lesson 23-1 Spanish Resources

Focus
- Write "What kinds of insurance do people generally have?" on the board. Discuss.

Teach
- What Is Insurance? (p. 343)
- Common Types of Insurance (pp. 343-345)
- Insurable Interest (pp. 345-346)
- What's Your Verdict? (pp. 343, 345)
- In This Case (pp. 343, 346)
- Curriculum Connection, *Communication* (TE, p. 344)
- Think Critically Through Visuals (TE, pp. 344, 345)

Apply
- Think About Legal Concepts 1-6 (p. 346)
- Think Critically About Evidence 7-10 (p. 346)

Assess
- Lesson 23-1 Quiz (Unit 4 Resource Book, p. 77)
- Reteach
Have students create a crossword puzzle using the following vocabulary words: *insurance, indemnity, insurer, insured, beneficiary, policy, face value, premium,* and *risk.*
- Enrich
Have pairs of students role-play being an insurance agent and client. The agent must use proper terminology to explain to the client what insurance is and why it is a practical necessity. The client should ask questions for clarification.

Close
- Conclude this lesson by stating that insurance is an arrangement for transferring and allocating risk. Most people insure their real and personal property, their lives, and their health to protect against loss.

Law for Business and Personal Use   Teacher: _____
                                             Week of: _____
                                               M   T   W   Th   F

Lesson 23-2   Property and Casualty Insurance Coverage
Pages 347-351

Goals
- Know the types of coverage provided by property and casualty insurance
- Understand the coverages provided in an automobile insurance policy

Teaching Resources
LAW LEARNING PACKAGE
- Student Activities and Study Guide, pp. 163-166
- Transparency 1
- Unit 4 Resource Book, pp. 81-84
- Lesson 23-2 Spanish Resources

Focus
- Separate students into groups of two or three. Ask them to brainstorm and write potential dangers to personal or real property, such as fire or theft. Make and display a composite list on the board when class begins. Discuss.

Teach
- Property and Casualty Insurance (pp. 347-349)
- Automobile Insurance (pp. 349-351)
- What's Your Verdict? (pp. 347, 349)
- Cultural Diversity in Law, *International* (p. 348)
- Curriculum Connection, *Math* (TE, p. 348)
- Think Critically Through Visuals (TE, pp. 349, 350)

Apply
- Think About Legal Concepts 1-5 (p. 351)
- Think Critically About Evidence 6-9 (p. 351)

Assess
- Lesson 23-2 Quiz (Unit 4 Resource Book, p. 81)
- Reteach
Have students write in their notebooks the boldfaced terms and definitions from this lesson.
- Enrich
  Have students debate the following question: "Should drivers in all states be required to obtain liability insurance before a driver's license is issued?"

Close
- Draw two columns on the board. Label the columns *Types* and *Coverage*. Under types, list the types of automobile insurance coverage that are available. Then write a brief description of the coverage for each type of insurance.

Law for Business and Personal Use   Teacher: _____
                                                       Week of: _____
                                                            M   T   W   Th   F

Lesson 23-3   Life and Social Insurance Coverage
            Pages 352-355

Goals
* Identify common provisions in life insurance contracts
* Explain the types of social insurance

Teaching Resources
LAW LEARNING PACKAGE
* Student Activities and Study Guide, pp. 167-168
* Transparencies 1, 2
* Unit 4 Resource Book, pp. 85-88
* Lesson 23-3 Spanish Resources

Focus
* Write "At your age, why do you think you should be concerned about life, social, and retirement insurance?" Discuss.

Teach
* Life and Social Insurance (p. 352)
* Life Insurance (pp. 352-353)
* Social Insurance (pp. 353-354)
* What's Your Verdict? (pp. 352, 353)
* A Question of Ethics (p. 353)
* Law and the Internet (p. 354)
* Curriculum Connection, *Social Studies* (TE, p. 354)

Apply
* Think About Legal Concepts 1-5 (p. 355)
* Think Critically About Evidence 6-8 (p. 355)

Assess
* Lesson 23-3 Quiz (Unit 4 Resource Book, p. 85)
* Reteach
Separate the class into four groups, one for each of the RSDHI programs. Have each group write a scenario describing three fictitious people who would qualify for that RSDHI program. Read and discuss each scenario.
* Enrich
Have students gather magazine and newspaper articles about various RSDHI programs, such as changes in laws, problems, fraud charges, and so on. Discuss the articles and have students create a bulletin board display.

Close
* Read and discuss *Prevent Legal Difficulties* on page 355. Have students brainstorm to add three more items to the list.

Law for Business and Personal Use

Chapter 23 in Review
Pages 356-359

Teaching Resources
LAW LEARNING PACKAGE
- Chapter 23 Test (Unit 4 Resource Book, pp. 89-90)
- Interactive Business Law Study Guide Chapter 23
- WESTEST Chapter 23

Review
- Concepts in Brief 1-8 (p. 356)
- Your Legal Vocabulary 1-12 (p. 356)
- Review Legal Concepts 13-17 (p. 357)
- Write About Legal Concepts 18-19 (p. 357)
- Think Critically About Evidence 20-24 (p. 357)
- Analyze Real Cases 25-31 (p. 358)

Apply
- Case for Legal Thinking (p. 359)
  - Practice Judging 1-3

Assess
- WESTEST Chapter 23
- Chapter 23 Test (Unit 4 Resource Book, pp. 89-90)

Law for Business and Personal Use

Teacher: _____

Week of: _____

M	T	W	Th	F

Chapter 24   **Wills, Estates, and Trusts**
                     pp. 360-373

Introduction
- Hot Debate (p. 360)

Chapter 24 Teaching Resources

LAW LEARNING PACKAGE
- Unit 4 Resource Book, pp. 95-104
- Transparencies 1, 2, 30, 31, 32, 33
- Student Activities and Study Guide, pp. 169-174
- Lessons 24-1 and 24-2 Spanish Resources
- Interactive Business Law Study Guide Chapter 24
- WESTEST Chapter 24

Law for Business and Personal Use   Teacher: _____
                                                        Week of: _____
                                                              M   T   W   Th   F

Lesson 24-1   Legal Consequences of Death
Pages 361-365

Goals
- Explain why an orderly distribution of a descendant's estate is necessary
- Discuss the benefits of making a will
- Describe how a valid will is made

Teaching Resources
LAW LEARNING PACKAGE
- Student Activities and Study Guide, pp. 169-172
- Transparencies 1, 30, 31, 32,
- Unit 4 Resource Book, pp. 95-98
- Lesson 24-1 Spanish Resources

Focus
- Ask students to name three reasons why they think a person should have a will. Discuss.

Teach
- Death and the Law (pp. 361-363)
- Distribution of a Decedent's Estate (pp. 363-364)
- What's Your Verdict? (pp. 361, 363)
- Cultural Diversity in Law, *Hawaii* (p. 364)
- In This Case (p. 363)
- Law in the Media (p. 364)
- Curriculum Connection, *Communication* (TE, p. 363)
- Think Critically Through Visuals (TE, p. 362)

Apply
- Think About Legal Concepts 1-8 (p. 365)
- Think Critically About Evidence 9-14 (p. 365)

Assess
- Lesson 24-1 Quiz (Unit 4 Resource Book, p. 95)
- Reteach
Have each student create a problem to illustrate per capita and per stirpes distributions. Have them draw
    an illustration of how their sample estate would be distributed under each method.
- Enrich
    Have students consider the consequences of using computer software and electronic data storage for
    preparing their own wills. Have students brainstorm and debate the issues that might arise from wills
    composed on the computer.

Close
- Separate the class into two groups and assign one of the two lesson sections to each group. Have
    each student think of one *Jeopardy*-style question for that section. After all questions are written, have
    each student ask his or her question while others write down their answers. When finished, have each
    student provide the question to his or her answer.

Law for Business and Personal Use

Teacher: _____

Week of: _____

M   T   W   Th   F

Lesson 24-2   Trusts
Pages 366-369

Goals
- Explain the usefulness of trusts
- Name and describe the various types of trusts
- Distinguish between express and implied trusts

Teaching Resources
LAW LEARNING PACKAGE
- Student Activities and Study Guide, pp. 173-174
- Transparencies 1, 2, 33
- Unit 4 Resource Book, pp. 99-102
- Lesson 24-2 Spanish Resources

Focus
- Read and discuss this scenario with the class:
    - Della and her husband, Charles, are concerned that when their children inherit the family farm, they will sell it and squander the proceeds within a short time. The parents think their children "simply do not know the value of a dollar." What can Della and Charles do to keep their children from squandering their inheritance?

Teach
- Creation of Trusts (pp. 366-367)
- Types of Trusts (p. 368)
- What's Your Verdict? (pp. 366, 368)
- A Question of Ethics (p. 368)
- Law and the Internet (p. 368)
- Think Critically Through Visuals (TE, p. 367)

Apply
- Think About Legal Concepts 1-9 (p. 369)
- Think Critically About Evidence 10-13 (p. 369)

Assess
- Lesson 24-2 Quiz (Unit 4 Resource Book, p. 99)
- Reteach
Have students make up five true or false statements with answers about the material in this lesson. Have them exchange papers and explain to each other why each statement is true or false.
- Enrich
Have students research a trust established for charitable purposes, including the amount of the endowment and what institutions benefit.

Close
- Review and make sure students can meet the lesson goals on page 366.
- Read and discuss *Prevent Legal Difficulties* on page 369.

Law for Business and Personal Use

Teacher: _____
Week of: _____

M	T	W	Th	F

Chapter 24 in Review
Pages 370-373

Teaching Resources
LAW LEARNING PACKAGE
- Chapter 24 Test (Unit 4 Resource Book, pp. 103-104)
- Interactive Business Law Study Guide Chapter 24
- WESTEST Chapter 24

Review
- Concepts in Brief 1-6 (p. 370)
- Your Legal Vocabulary 1-15 (p. 370)
- Review Legal Concepts 16-22 (p. 371)
- Write About Legal Concepts 23-26 (p. 371)
- Think Critically About Evidence 27-31 (p. 371)
- Analyze Real Cases 32-38 (p. 372)

Apply
- Case for Legal Thinking (p. 373)
  - Practice Judging 1-3

Assess
- WESTEST Chapter 24
- Chapter 24 Test (Unit 4 Resource Book, pp. 103-104)

Unit 4 Property   (Chapters 19-24)
pp. 280-375
Wrap-Up
- Entrepreneurs and the Law (pp. 374-375)
  - Project 4   Property
  - Think Critically Through Visuals (TE, p. 375)

Law for Business and Personal Use

Teacher: _____
Week of: _____
M   T   W   Th   F

Unit 5 The Law of Jobs   (Chapters 25-30)
pp. 376-465

Introduction
- In Practice Profile: Sharon Lamm, Human Resource Specialist (p. 377)

Chapter 25   Chapter of Agency
pp. 378-389

Introduction
- Hot Debate (p. 378)

Chapter 25 Teaching Resources
LAW LEARNING PACKAGE
- Unit 5 Resource Book, pp. 5-14
- Transparencies 1, 23, 35, 36
- Student Activities and Study Guide, pp. 175-178
- Lessons 25-1 and 25-2 Spanish Resources
- Interactive Business Law Study Guide Chapter 25
- WESTEST Chapter 25

Law for Business and Personal Use

Teacher: _____
Week of: _____

M   T   W   Th   F

Lesson 25-1   Overview of Agency
Pages 379-381

Goals
- Describe when an agency relationship exists
- Identify who is qualified to be a principal and who is qualified to be an agent
- Discuss how the law treats principals and agents who lack contractual capacity

Teaching Resources
LAW LEARNING PACKAGE
- Student Activities and Study Guide, pp. 175-176
- Transparencies 1, 35
- Unit 5 Resource Book, pp. 5-8
- Lesson 25-1 Spanish Resources

Focus
- Have small groups of students brainstorm and make a list of as many types of agents as they can. Discuss.

Teach
- What Is an Agency Relationship? (pp. 379-380)
- Who Can Be a Principal? (p. 380)
- Who Can Be an Agent? (p. 381)
- What's Your Verdict? (pp. 379, 380, 381)
- In This Case (pp. 379, 380)
- Curriculum Connection, *Communications* (TE, p. 379)
- Think Critically Through Visuals (TE, p. 380)

Apply
- Think About Legal Concepts 1-3 (p. 381)
- Think Critically About Evidence 4-5 (p. 381)

Assess
- Lesson 25-1 Quiz (Unit 5 Resource Book, p. 5)
- Reteach
Have students draw a diagram, such as the one on page 380, to show a specific agency relationship of their choosing.
- Enrich
Have students write a short essay about the following: Contract law assumes that all parties will look out for their own self-interests, whereas agency law requires the agent to look out for the best interests of the principal. Why do you think these bodies of law have such different orientations?

Close
- Distribute to small groups newspaper ads, "junk mail" flyers, and the "Yellow Pages" from the telephone directory. Have students examine the material and make lists of agency relationships that they find.

Law for Business and Personal Use

Teacher: _____

Week of: _____

M   T   W   Th   F

Lesson 25-2   Scope of Agency Authority
Pages 382-385

Goals
* Identify the sources of an agent's authority
* Describe the acts of an agent which bind the principal
* Explain what happens when an agent acts outside the scope of express authority

Teaching Resources
LAW LEARNING PACKAGE
* Student Activities and Study Guide, pp. 177-178
* Transparencies 1, 2, 36
* Unit 5 Resource Book, pp. 9-12
* Lesson 25-2 Spanish Resources

Focus
* Have students define the word *attorney*. Then read aloud the definition of *attorney* from *The American Heritage Dictionary*. "A person legally appointed or empowered to act for another." Discuss.

Teach
* Creation of Agency Authority (pp. 382-384)
* What's Your Verdict? (p. 382)
* Cultural Diversity in Law, *International* (p. 384)
* In This Case (p. 384)
* A Question of Ethics (p. 384)
* Curriculum Connection, *Language Arts* (TE, p. 383)
* Think Critically Through Visuals (TE, p. 382)

Apply
* Think About Legal Concepts 1-5 (p. 385)
* Think Critically About Evidence 6-8 (p. 385)

Assess
* Lesson 25-2 Quiz (Unit 5 Resource Book, p. 9)
* Reteach
Write *gratuitous agency, express authority, power of attorney, implied authority, apparent authority,* and *ratification* on the board. Ask each student to copy the terms and define each term in their own words in their notebooks.
* Enrich
Provide students with newspapers and magazines to create a bulletin-board display made up of ads or articles that describe various types of agency authority. Have them label each type of authority described.

Close
* Separate the class into three groups. Assign each group one of the points in *Prevent Legal Difficulties* on page 385. Have each group prepare a presentation of the point and share it with the class.

Law for Business and Personal Use

Teacher: _____
Week of: _____
        M   T   W   Th   F

Chapter 25 in Review
Pages 386-389

Teaching Resources
LAW LEARNING PACKAGE
- Chapter 25 Test (Unit 5 Resource Book, pp. 13-14)
- Interactive Business Law Study Guide Chapter 25
- WESTEST Chapter 25

Review
- Concepts in Brief 1-11 (p. 386)
- Your Legal Vocabulary 1-12 (p. 386)
- Review Legal Concepts 13-16 (p. 387)
- Write About Legal Concepts 17-20 (p. 387)
- Think Critically About Evidence 21-24 (p. 387)
- Analyze Real Cases 25-31 (p. 388)

Apply
- Case for Legal Thinking (p. 389)
  - Practice Judging 1-2

Assess
- WESTEST Chapter 25
- Chapter 25 Test (Unit 5 Resource Book, pp.13-14)

Law for Business and Personal Use

Chapter 26   Operation of Agency
pp. 390-401

Introduction
- Hot Debate (p. 390)

Chapter 26 Teaching Resources
LAW LEARNING PACKAGE
- Unit 5 Resource Book, pp. 19-28
- Transparencies 1, 2
- Student Activities and Study Guide, pp. 179-182
- Lessons 26-1 and 26-2 Spanish Resources
- Interactive Business Law Study Guide Chapter 26
- WESTEST Chapter 26

Law for Business and Personal Use

Lesson 26-1   Agent's Fiduciary Duties
Pages 391-393

Goals
- Describe each fiduciary duty of an agent
- Identify when each fiduciary duty has been violated
- Explain the principal's remedies for an agent's violation of a fiduciary duty

Teaching Resources
LAW LEARNING PACKAGE
- Student Activities and Study Guide, pp. 179-180
- Transparencies 1, 2
- Unit 5 Resource Book, pp. 19-22
- Lesson 26-1 Spanish Resources

Focus
- Read aloud to the class the scenario in the FOCUS section of the TE on page 391. Discuss.

Teach
- What Are an Agent's Fiduciary Duties? (pp. 391-392)
- What's Your Verdict? (p. 391)
- In This Case (pp. 391, 392)
- A Question of Ethics (p. 392)
- FYI (p. 392)
- Curriculum Connection, *Communication* (TE, p. 392)
- Think Critically Through Visuals (TE, p. 391)

Apply
- Think About Legal Concepts 1-7 (p. 393)
- Think Critically About Evidence 8-13 (p. 393)

Assess
- Lesson 26-1 Quiz (Unit 5 Resource Book, p. 19)
- Reteach
Have students write five quiz questions based on the information in this lesson. Have students exchange
    papers and take each other's quizzes.
- Enrich
    Have students brainstorm and write a list of agency relationships in which the duty of reasonable care
    and skill is particularly important.

Close
- Review the *FYI* feature on page 392.

Law for Business and Personal Use

Teacher: _____

Week of: _____

M   T   W   Th   F

Lesson 26-2   Other Liabilities in Agency
Pages 394-397

Goals
- Describe a principal's liabilities
- Describe an agent's liabilities

Teaching Resources
LAW LEARNING PACKAGE
- Student Activities and Study Guide, pp. 181-182
- Transparency 1
- Unit 5 Resource Book, pp. 23-26
- Lesson 26-2 Spanish Resources

Focus
- Have a student read *What's Your Verdict* on page 394. Discuss.

Teach
- When Is a Principal Liable? (p. 394)
- When Is an Agent Liable to Third Persons? (p. 395)
- How Is an Agency Terminated? (pp. 395-396)
- What's Your Verdict? (pp. 394, 395)
- Cultural Diversity in Law, *International* (p. 396)
- In This Case (pp. 394, 395)
- Curriculum Connection, *Science/Health* (TE, p. 395)
- Think Critically Through Visuals (TE, p. 394)

Apply
- Think About Legal Concepts 1-3 (p. 397)
- Think Critically About Evidence 4-8 (p. 397)

Assess
- Lesson 26-2 Quiz (Unit 5 Resource Book, p. 23)
- Reteach
Have students create a graphic illustration of both a principal's and an agent's liability to third persons.
- Enrich
  Have students interpret the phrase "having the power, but not the right" (on page 395) in a short essay.

Close
- Separate the class into three groups. Assign each group either principal, third person, or agent. Have each group present to the class an oral summarization of the points in *Prevent Legal Difficulties* on page 397 relating to their party.

Law for Business and Personal Use

Chapter 26 in Review
Pages 398-401

Teaching Resources

LAW LEARNING PACKAGE
- Chapter 26 Test (Unit 5 Resource Book, pp. 27-28)
- Interactive Business Law Study Guide Chapter 26
- WESTEST Chapter 26

Review
- Concepts in Brief 1-10 (p. 398)
- Your Legal Vocabulary 1-10 (p. 398)
- Review Legal Concepts 11-14 (p. 399)
- Write About Legal Concepts 15-18 (p. 399)
- Think Critically About Evidence 19-23 (p. 399)
- Analyze Real Cases 24-27 (p. 400)

Apply
- Case for Legal Thinking (p. 401)
  - Practice Judging 1-2

Assess
- WESTEST Chapter 26
- Chapter 26 Test (Unit 5 Resource Book, pp. 27-28)

Law for Business and Personal Use

Teacher: _____

Week of: _____

            M   T   W   Th   F

Chapter 27   Employment Contracts
pp. 402-417

Introduction
- Hot Debate (p. 402)

Chapter 27 Teaching Resources
LAW LEARNING PACKAGE
- Unit 5 Resource Book, pp. 33-46
- Transparencies 1, 2
- Student Activities and Study Guide, pp. 183-190
- Lessons 27-1, 27-2, and 27-3 Spanish Resources
- Interactive Business Law Study Guide Chapter 27
- WESTEST Chapter 27

Law for Business and Personal Use

Teacher: _____

Week of: _____

M   T   W   Th   F

Lesson 27-1   Creation of Employment Contracts
Pages 403-406

Goals
- Define employment and contrast it with other relationships where one person works for another
- Describe how the *terms* in employment contracts are created
- Discuss the duties imposed by law on employees

Teaching Resources
LAW LEARNING PACKAGE
- Student Activities and Study Guide, pp. 183-186
- Transparencies 1, 2
- Unit 5 Resource Book, pp. 33-36
- Lesson 27-1 Spanish Resources

Focus
- Write "Name any paying jobs you have held and identify the responsibilities that accompanied each job." Discuss.

Teach
- What Is Employment? (p. 403)
- Terms of the Employment Contract (pp. 403-404)
- Employee Duties (p. 405)
- What's Your Verdict? (pp. 403, 405)
- In This Case (p. 405)
- A Question of Ethics (p. 404)
- Curriculum Connection, *History* (TE, p. 405)
- Think Critically Through Visuals (TE, pp. 402, 404)

Apply
- Think About Legal Concepts 1-7 (p. 406)
- Think Critically About Evidence 8-14 (p. 406)

Assess
- Lesson 27-1 Quiz (Unit 5 Resource Book, p. 33)
- Reteach
Ask students to identify whether the following are likely to be employees (E) or independent contractors (I): a house painter, in relation to the owner of the house (I); store manager (E); teacher (E); freelance photographer (I).
- Enrich
Have students write and perform two scenarios: one describing an employee-employer relationship and the other describing an independent contract-client relationship. Ask students to identify each other's scenarios.

Close
- Review the lesson goals on page 403. Make sure students can meet each of these goals.

Law for Business and Personal Use

Teacher: _____

Week of: _____

M   T   W   Th   F

Lesson 27-2   Employer's Basic Duties
Pages 407-410

Goals
* Describe the employer's duties that arise out of the express terms of the employment contract
* Explain the employer's duties imposed by law

Teaching Resources
LAW LEARNING PACKAGE
* Student Activities and Study Guide, pp. 187-188
* Transparency 1
* Unit 5 Resource Book, pp. 37-40
* Lesson 27-2 Spanish Resources

Focus
* Have students make a list of what duties they think the school should owe to them as students. Have them list corresponding duties they owe to the school and their teachers. Discuss.

Teach
* Employer's Duties to Employees (pp. 407-409)
* Employer's Duty to Those Injured by Employees (p. 409)
* What's Your Verdict? (pp. 407, 409)
* Cultural Diversity in Law, *Mexico* (p. 409)
* In This Case (p. 407)
* FYI (p. 409)
* Curriculum Connection, *Health* (TE, p. 407)
* Think Critically Through Visuals (TE, p. 408)

Apply
* Think About Legal Concepts 1-7 (p. 410)
* Think Critically About Evidence 8-13 (p. 410)

Assess
* Lesson 27-2 Quiz (Unit 5 Resource Book, p. 37)
* Reteach
Have students identify in writing the duties imposed by law on employers and explain why these duties exist.
* Enrich
Have groups of students write scenarios dealing with an employer's liability for the torts of its employees. In the first scenario, the employer should be liable; in the second, the employer should not be liable.

Close
* Review the employer's duties to employees and to third parties injured by employees.

Law for Business and Personal Use   Teacher: _____
                                                       Week of: _____
                                                              M   T   W   Th   F

Lesson 27-3   Termination of Employment Contracts
Pages 411-413

Goals
- Tell when an employee is liable for quitting a job
- Describe when an employer is liable for firing an employee
- Explain the rights of a fired employee

Teaching Resources
LAW LEARNING PACKAGE
- Student Activities and Study Guide, pp. 189-190
- Transparencies 1, 2
- Unit 5 Resource Book, pp. 41-44
- Lesson 27-3 Spanish Resources

Focus
- Ask students if they think there is any difference in employees' rights in termination of employment contracts with the government versus the private sector. Discuss.

Teach
- Types of Employment Contracts (pp. 411-412)
- What's Your Verdict? (p. 411)
- In This Case (p. 412)
- A Question of Ethics (p. 412)
- Curriculum Connection, *Communication* (TE, p. 412)

Apply
- Think About Legal Concepts 1-4 (p. 413)
- Think Critically About Evidence 5-8 (p. 413)

Assess
- Lesson 27-3 Quiz (Unit 5 Resource Book, p. 41)
- Reteach
Have a peer-tutor create a scenario covering the material in this lesson. Pair this student with another who needs reteaching and have him or her identify the main points.
- Enrich
Have students contact the local office of your state's unemployment commission for flyers, bulletins, or pamphlets on unemployment compensation rights. Have students find out when one is eligible, how to apply, and how payments are made.

Close
- Separate the class into five groups. Assign each group one of the points in *Prevent Legal Difficulties* on page 413. Ask each group to prepare and present to the class a poster summarizing the point they were assigned.

Law for Business and Personal Use

Chapter 27 in Review
Pages 414-417

Teaching Resources
LAW LEARNING PACKAGE
- Chapter 27 Test (Unit 5 Resource Book, pp. 45-46)
- Interactive Business Law Study Guide Chapter 27
- WESTEST Chapter 27

Review
- Concepts in Brief 1-7 (p. 414)
- Your Legal Vocabulary 1-12 (p. 414)
- Review Legal Concepts 13-16 (p. 415)
- Write About Legal Concepts 17-20 (p. 415)
- Think Critically About Evidence 21-24 (p. 415)
- Analyze Real Cases 25-30 (p. 416)

Apply
- Case for Legal Thinking (p. 417)
  - Practice Judging 1-2

Assess
- WESTEST Chapter 27
- Chapter 27 Test (Unit 5 Resource Book, pp. 45-46)

Law for Business and Personal Use

Teacher: _____

Week of: _____

     M   T   W   Th   F

Chapter 28   Unions
pp. 418-431

Introduction
- Hot Debate (p. 418)

Chapter 28 Teaching Resources
LAW LEARNING PACKAGE
- Unit 5 Resource Book, pp. 51-60
- Transparencies 1, 2, 37, 38
- Student Activities and Study Guide, pp. 191-198
- Lessons 28-1 and 28-2 Spanish Resources
- Interactive Business Law Study Guide Chapter 28
- WESTEST Chapter 28

Law for Business and Personal Use

Lesson 28-1   How Are Unions Established?
Pages 419-421

Goals
* Explain the roles of state and federal labor laws
* Describe the history of labor law
* Discuss the processes for establishing a new union, changing unions, and eliminating union representation

Teaching Resources
LAW LEARNING PACKAGE
* Student Activities and Study Guide, pp. 191-194
* Transparencies 1, 2
* Unit 5 Resource Book, pp. 51-54
* Lesson 28-1 Spanish Resources

Focus
* Tell students that the early history of the labor movement could not be told without mentioning the struggles of the coal miners to unionize. Ask students if they think the concerns of coal miners today differ from the concerns of miners in their early days of organizing.

Teach
* State and Federal Regulation of Employment (p. 419)
* History of Labor Laws (p. 419)
* The National Labor Relations Board (p. 420)
* How Are Unions Established? (pp. 420-421)
* What's Your Verdict? (pp. 419, 420)
* A Question of Ethics (p. 421, TE p. 420)
* Curriculum Connection, *History* (TE, p. 420)

Apply
* Think About Legal Concepts 1-6 (p. 421)
* Think Critically About Evidence 7-10 (p. 421)

Assess
* Lesson 28-1 Quiz (Unit 5 Resource Book, p. 51)
* Reteach
Have students use the seven boldfaced terms introduced in this lesson to create a crossword puzzle and answer key. Have students exchange papers and complete the puzzle.
* Enrich
Have students put themselves in Joyce's situation in *What's Your Verdict?* at the tope of page 420. Ask students to write a written complaint to file with the NLRB. Display students' work on a bulletin board.

Close
* Review the lesson goals on page 419. Be sure all students can meet each of these goals.

Law for Business and Personal Use   Teacher: _____
                                                       Week of: _____
                                                       M   T   W   Th   F

Lesson 28-2   Relations in a Unionized Workplace
Pages 422-427

Goals
- Explain how union certification affects employees
- Discuss unfair labor practices by unions and management

Teaching Resources
LAW LEARNING PACKAGE
- Student Activities and Study Guide, pp. 195-198
- Transparencies 1, 37, 38
- Unit 5 Resource Book, pp. 55-58
- Lesson 28-2 Spanish Resources

Focus
- Begin class with the following quotation of Samuel Gompers, an American labor leader who lived from 1850 to 1924: "Show me the country in which there are no strikes, and I'll show you the country in which there is no liberty." Discuss.

Teach
- Union Certification (p. 422)
- Collective Bargaining (p. 423)
- Unfair Practices by Management (p. 424)
- What Are Unfair Labor Practices by Unions? (p. 425)
- When May Unions Strike? (p.426)
- When May a Union Boycott? (p. 426)
- What's Your Verdict? (pp. 422, 423, 424, 425, 426)
- Cultural Diversity in Law, *Mexico* (p. 426)
- In This Case (p. 424)
- Curriculum Connection, *Math* (TE, p. 424)
- Think Critically Through Visuals (TE, pp. 423, 425)

Apply
- Think About Legal Concepts 1-3 (p. 427)
- Think Critically About Evidence 4-6 (p. 427)

Assess
- Lesson 28-2 Quiz (Unit 5 Resource Book, p. 55)
- Reteach
Separate the class into two groups. Have one group create an illustrative poster to alert workers to unfair labor practices by management. Have the other group alert management to unfair labor practices by unions.
- Enrich
Have one group of students represent labor or union members and the other group represent management. Have students role-play or discuss collective bargaining over the issue of safety in the workplace. If necessary, the instructor can role-play the mediator.

Close
- Have students create mobiles to illustrate the items in *Prevent Legal Difficulties* on page 427. Students may use pictures from newspapers, magazines, clip-art software, or drawings.

Law for Business and Personal Use

Chapter 28 in Review
Pages 428-431

Teaching Resources
LAW LEARNING PACKAGE
* Chapter 28 Test (Unit 5 Resource Book, pp. 59-60)
* Interactive Business Law Study Guide Chapter 28
* WESTEST Chapter 28

Review
* Concepts in Brief 1-7 (p. 428)
* Your Legal Vocabulary 1-10 (p. 428)
* Review Legal Concepts 11-18 (p. 429)
* Write About Legal Concepts 19-22 (p. 429)
* Think Critically About Evidence 23-27 (p. 429)
* Analyze Real Cases 28-32 (p. 430)

Apply
* Case for Legal Thinking (p. 431)
    * Practice Judging 1-3

Assess
* WESTEST Chapter 28
* Chapter 28 Test (Unit 5 Resource Book, pp. 59-60)

Law for Business and Personal Use

Teacher: _____
Week of: _____

M   T   W   Th   F

Chapter 29   Employment Discrimination
pp. 432-447

Introduction
- Hot Debate (p. 432)

Chapter 29 Teaching Resources

LAW LEARNING PACKAGE
- Unit 5 Resource Book, pp. 63-76
- Transparencies 1, 2,
- Student Activities and Study Guide, pp. 199-206
- Lessons 29-1, 29-2, and 29-3 Spanish Resources
- Interactive Business Law Study Guide Chapter 29
- WESTEST Chapter 29

Law for Business and Personal Use   Teacher: _____

Week of: _____

M   T   W   Th   F

Lesson 29-1   **Illegal Employment Discrimination**
                     Pages 433-435

Goals
- Define illegal discrimination
- Define legal discrimination
- Identify members of protected classes

Teaching Resources

LAW LEARNING PACKAGE
- Student Activities and Study Guide, pp. 199-200
- Transparency 1
- Unit 5 Resource Book, pp. 63-66
- Lesson 29-1 Spanish Resources

Focus
- Write the following on the board:
    1. A male employer hires only women because he thinks they are better employees
    2. A female employer hires only women because she thinks women are usually discriminated against
    3. An employer hires only women who are past the childbearing age
    4. An employer hires only people under age 40
- Ask students which are examples of illegal discrimination. (all are) Discuss.

Teach
- Unjustified Discrimination (p. 433)
- Types of Unjustified Discrimination (p. 434)
- The Scope of Protection (pp. 434-435)
- What's Your Verdict? (pp. 433, 434)
- Cultural Diversity in Law, *European Union* (p. 435)
- Curriculum Connection, *Physical Education* (TE, p. 434)
- Think Critically Through Visuals (TE, p. 433)

Apply
- Think About Legal Concepts 1-5 (p. 435)
- Think Critically About Evidence 6-9 (p. 435)

Assess
- Lesson 29-1 Quiz (Unit 5 Resource Book, p. 63)
- Reteach

Have each student make a two-column chart with headings "Justified" and "Unjustified." Have students list examples of justified and unjustified discrimination in the workplace. Make a class list on the board.
- Enrich

Have each student clip from a magazine an illustration of a member of a protected class. Have each student write an explanation of why an employer who discriminates against the pictured person would be acting unethically and illegally.

Close
- Review the questions in *What's Your Verdict?* on pages 433 and 434.

Law for Business and Personal Use   Teacher: _____
                                                   Week of: _____
                                                   M   T   W   Th   F

Lesson 29-2   Proving Illegal Discrimination
Pages 436-440

Goals
* Explain how unequal treatment can be proved
* Identify employers' major defenses in discrimination suits
* Explain what constitutes sexual harassment

Teaching Resources
LAW LEARNING PACKAGE
* Student Activities and Study Guide, pp. 201-204
* Transparencies 1, 2
* Unit 5 Resource Book, pp. 67-70
* Lesson 29-2 Spanish Resources

Focus
* Ask a student volunteer to read *What's Your Verdict?* on page 436. Discuss.

Teach
* How Can Unequal Treatment Be Proved? (pp. 436-437)
* What Is Disparate Impact? (p. 438)
* Proving Pattern and Practice of Discrimination (p. 439)
* Sexual Harassment (p. 439)
* What's Your Verdict? (pp. 436, 438, 439)
* In This Case (pp. 436, 437, 438)
* A Question of Ethics (p. 439)
* Curriculum Connection, *Math* (TE, p. 438)
* Think Critically Through Visuals (TE, pp. 437, 439)

Apply
* Think About Legal Concepts 1-7 (p. 440)
* Think Critically About Evidence 8-13 (p. 440)

Assess
* Lesson 29-2 Quiz (Unit 5 Resource Book, p. 67)
* Reteach
On the board, list four factors an employee must show to establish intent by indirect evidence in a
    discrimination case. Have students create examples of such discrimination.
* Enrich
    Have students research the current percentage of the U.S. population within each of the following
    groups: Anglo-American, African-American, Native-American, Asian-American, and Hispanic-
    American.

Close
* Review the vocabulary terms in this lesson.

Law for Business and Personal Use

Teacher: _____
Week of: _____

M   T   W   Th   F

Lesson 29-3   Specific Laws Making Unjustified Discrimination Illegal
Pages 441-443

Goals
- Describe the Civil Rights Act of 1964
- Name the laws which make discrimination on the basis of age, pregnancy, and disability illegal

Teaching Resources
LAW LEARNING PACKAGE
- Student Activities and Study Guide, pp. 205-206
- Transparency 1
- Unit 5 Resource Book, pp. 71-74
- Lesson 29-3 Spanish Resources

Focus
- Read the following example to the class: "River City Supply Co. hires several stock clerks to help maintain the stock room, put goods on store shelves, and help customers load purchased goods into their vehicles. If a clerk suffers a minor injury to his back or leg and is unable to lift, but can otherwise work, River City gives the worker light duty until the condition heals. The worker may do inventory counting, watch goods in high-theft areas, and so forth. The Pregnancy Discrimination Act would require that the store give a pregnant worker the same allowance for her condition during pregnancy."
- Ask students if they think pregnancy discrimination is a form of discrimination against women or a form of discrimination against families.

Teach
- Legislation Prohibiting Discrimination (pp. 441-442)
- What's Your Verdict? (p. 441)
- Law in the Media (p. 442)
- Curriculum Connection, *Communication* (TE, p. 441)
- Think Critically Through Visuals (TE, p. 442)

Apply
- Think About Legal Concepts 1-3 (p. 443)
- Think Critically About Evidence 4-7 (p. 443)

Assess
- Lesson 29-3 Quiz (Unit 5 Resource Book, p. 71)
- Reteach
Have each pair of students explain to the class one of the five federal laws prohibiting discrimination as discussed in this lesson. Make sure the correct information is disseminated.
- Enrich
Have students research current periodicals for cases of discrimination. Have students write a one-page report on a case, highlighting the important facts of the incident.

Close
- Read and discuss *Prevent Legal Difficulties* on page 443.

Law for Business and Personal Use

Teacher: _____

Week of: _____

M   T   W   Th   F

Chapter 29 in Review
Pages 444-447

Teaching Resources

LAW LEARNING PACKAGE

- Chapter 29 Test (Unit 5 Resource Book, pp. 75-76)
- Interactive Business Law Study Guide Chapter 29
- WESTEST Chapter 29

Review

- Concepts in Brief 1-9 (p. 444)
- Your Legal Vocabulary 1-10 (p. 444)
- Review Legal Concepts 11-14 (p. 445)
- Write About Legal Concepts 15-17 (p. 445)
- Think Critically About Evidence 18-21 (p. 445)
- Analyze Real Cases 22-27 (p. 446)

Apply

- Case for Legal Thinking (p. 447)
  - Practice Judging 1-2

Assess

- WESTEST Chapter 29
- Chapter 29 Test (Unit 5 Resource Book, pp. 75-76)

Law for Business and Personal Use

Teacher: _____

Week of: _____

          M   T   W   Th   F

Chapter 30   Employee Injuries
pp. 448-463

Introduction

- Hot Debate (p. 448)

Chapter 30 Teaching Resources

LAW LEARNING PACKAGE

- Unit 5 Resource Book, pp. 81-94
- Transparencies 1, 2
- Student Activities and Study Guide, pp. 207-212
- Lessons 30-1, 30-2, and 30-3 Spanish Resources
- Interactive Business Law Study Guide Chapter 30
- WESTEST Chapter 30

Law for Business and Personal Use

Lesson 30-1   Employer's Tort Liability
Pages 449-451

Goals
- Discuss the relationship among negligence suits, workers' compensation, and OSHA
- Explain when the employer is liable to the injured employee

Teaching Resources
LAW LEARNING PACKAGE
- Student Activities and Study Guide, pp. 207-208
- Transparency 1
- Unit 5 Resource Book, pp. 81-84
- Lesson 30-1 Spanish Resources

Focus
- Take the survey as described under FOCUS on page 449 of the Teacher's Edition.
- Save the results for discussion at the closure of Lesson 30-3. (See TE p. 459)

Teach
- Introduction to Job Safety (pp. 449-450)
- Recovering from the Employer for Negligence (pp. 450-451)
- What's Your Verdict? (pp. 449, 450)
- FYI (p. 451)
- Curriculum Connection, *Language Arts* (TE, p. 449)
- Think Critically Through Visuals (TE, p. 450)

Apply
- Think About Legal Concepts 1-2 (p. 451)
- Think Critically About Evidence 3-5 (p. 451)

Assess
- Lesson 30-1 Quiz (Unit 5 Resource Book, p. 81)
- Reteach
Have students outline this lesson in their notebooks. Make sure they include the three ways our legal
   system deals with employee injuries and also the common law defenses.
- Enrich
   Have students clip articles from newspapers about injuries to employees. Have them read and orally
   summarize the activities. Have the class determine which worker-protection approach might play a
   role in the case.

Close
- Review questions in *What's Your Verdict?* on pages 449 and 450.

Law for Business and Personal Use

Teacher: _____

Week of: _____

M   T   W   Th   F

Lesson 30-2   Workers' Compensation
Pages 452-455

Goals
- Determine the injuries for which workers' compensation is liable
- Describe the defenses available to workers' compensation insurers
- Identify employees who need not be covered by workers' compensation

Teaching Resources
LAW LEARNING PACKAGE
- Student Activities and Study Guide, pp. 209-210
- Transparencies 1, 2
- Unit 5 Resource Book, pp. 85-88
- Lesson 30-2 Spanish Resources

Focus
- Have students recall and share incidents that they have experienced or witnessed involving injuries in school or at work.

Teach
- Operation of Workers' Compensation (pp. 452-453)
- Injuries Covered (pp. 453-454)
- Who Is Not Covered? (pp. 454-455)
- What's Your Verdict? (pp. 452, 453, 454)
- In This Case (pp. 452, 453, 454)
- A Question of Ethics (p. 454)
- Curriculum Connection, *Economics* (TE, p. 453)
- Think Critically Through Visuals (TE, p. 454)

Apply
- Think About Legal Concepts 1-4 (p. 455)
- Think Critically About Evidence 5-8 (p. 455)

Assess
- Lesson 30-2 Quiz (Unit 5 Resource Book, p. 85)
- Reteach
Make a two-column chart on the board. Label the columns: *Covered Employees* and *Employees Not Covered.* Have students give examples for each column.
- Enrich
Have students debate the workers' compensation standard practice of adjusting the amount of benefit for vocational rehabilitation when either the employee or the employer is found to have been grossly negligent.

Close
- Review questions in *What's Your Verdict?* on pages 452, 453, 454.

Law for Business and Personal Use   Teacher: _____
                                                   Week of: _____
                                                   M   T   W   Th   F

Lesson 30-3   How Does OSHA Protect Employees?
Pages 456-459

Goals
- Name two ways OSHA protects employees
- Explain how OSHA obtains employer compliance with its requirements

Teaching Resources
LAW LEARNING PACKAGE
- Student Activities and Study Guide, pp. 211-212
- Transparencies 1, 2
- Unit 5 Resource Book, pp. 89-92
- Lesson 30-3 Spanish Resources

Focus
- Lead a discussion about César Estrada Chávez. (See FOCUS on page on page 456 of the Teacher's Edition for details.)

Teach
- How Does OSHA Protect Employees? (pp. 456-458)
- What's Your Verdict? (p. 456)
- Cultural Diversity in Law, *Canada* (p. 457)
- A Question of Ethics (p. 456)
- FYI (p. 456)
- Curriculum Connection, *Health* (TE, p. 458)
- Think Critically Through Visuals (TE, p. 457)

Apply
- Think About Legal Concepts 1-4 (p. 459)
- Think Critically About Evidence 5-7 (p. 459)

Assess
- Lesson 30-3 Quiz (Unit 5 Resource Book, p. 89)
- Reteach
Have small groups make flowcharts on blank overhead transparencies. The flowcharts should trace examples (fictitious or real) of workplace safety violations, from violation to OSHA action.
- Enrich
Have students write an essay in which they imagine what working conditions would be like if OSHA did not exist.

Close
- Read and discuss *Prevent Legal Difficulties* on page 459.
- Poll the students again to find out if their answers to the questions in the Focus activity on page 449 (lesson 30-1) have changed. Tally their responses and compare them with those from the beginning of this chapter. Discuss any differences.

Law for Business and Personal Use

Teacher: _____
Week of: _____
     M   T   W   Th   F

Chapter 30 in Review
Pages 460-463

Teaching Resources
LAW LEARNING PACKAGE
- Chapter 30 Test (Unit 5 Resource Book, pp. 93-94)
- Interactive Business Law Study Guide Chapter 30
- WESTEST Chapter 30

Review
- Concepts in Brief 1-8 (p. 460)
- Your Legal Vocabulary 1-10 (p. 460)
- Review Legal Concepts 11-13 (p. 461)
- Write About Legal Concepts 14-17 (p. 461)
- Think Critically About Evidence 18-21 (p. 461)
- Analyze Real Cases 22-26 (p. 462)

Apply
- Case for Legal Thinking (p. 463)
  - Practice Judging 1-2

Assess
- WESTEST Chapter 30
- Chapter 30 Test (Unit 5 Resource Book, pp. 93-94)

Unit 5 The Law of Jobs   (Chapters 25-30)
pp. 376-465
Wrap-Up
- Entrepreneurs and the Law (pp. 464-465)
  - Project 5 The Law of Jobs
  - Think Critically Through Visuals (TE, p. 465)

Law for Business and Personal Use   Teacher: _____
                                                   Week of: _____
                                                            M   T   W   Th   F

Unit 6 Forms of Business Organizations   (Chapters 31-34)
pp. 466-535

Introduction

- In Practice Profile: Richard Nella, Entrepreneur (p. 467)

Chapter 31   Forms of Business Organization
pp. 468-487

Introduction

- Hot Debate (p. 468)

Chapter 31 Teaching Resources

LAW LEARNING PACKAGE

- Unit 6 Resource Book, pp. 5-18
- Transparencies 1, 2, 40, 41
- Student Activities and Study Guide, pp. 5-16
- Lessons 31-1, 31-2, and 31-3 Spanish Resources
- Interactive Business Law Study Guide Chapter 31
- WESTEST Chapter 31

Law for Business and Personal Use

Teacher: _____

Week of: _____

M   T   W   Th   F

Lesson 31-1   Basic Attributes of Business Organizations
Pages 469-472

Goals

- Discuss the basic attributes of the sole proprietorship, partnership, and corporation
- Determine which one form of organization may be best in a particular situation
- Explain the risks of utilizing each form of business organization

Teaching Resources

LAW LEARNING PACKAGE

- Student Activities and Study Guide, pp. 213-214
- Transparencies 1, 2, 40
- Unit 6 Resource Book, pp. 5-8
- Lesson 31-1 Spanish Resources

Focus

- Create two columns on the board. Label one: "Why I want to go into business for myself." Label the other: "Why I don't want to go into business for myself." Have students contribute to the class list as well as make their own list in their notebooks.

Teach

- What Is a Sole Proprietorship? (p. 469)
- What Is a Partnership? (pp. 469-470)
- What Is a Corporation? (pp. 470-471)
- What's Your Verdict? (pp. 469, 470)
- A Question of Ethics (p. 471)
- Think Critically Through Visuals (TE, pp. 470, 471)

Apply

- Think About Legal Concepts 1-8 (p. 472)
- Think Critically About Evidence 9-15 (p. 472)

Assess

- Lesson 31-1 Quiz (Unit 6 Resource Book, p. 5)
- Reteach

Have students create a graphic organizer that illustrates the three forms of business organization and attributes of each.

- Enrich

Have students create and manage a daily bulletin board of articles dealing with business. Articles should be divided into the three forms of business organization.

Close

- Review questions in *What's Your Verdict?* on pages 469 and 470.

Law for Business and Personal Use   Teacher: _____

                                                       Week of: _____
                                                          M   T   W   Th   F

Lesson 31-2   Creating and Terminating Partnerships
Pages 473-478

Goals
*   Explain how a partnership is formed
*   Identify different types of partnerships and partners
*   Discuss the ways in which a partnership can be terminated and what happens when this occurs

Teaching Resources
LAW LEARNING PACKAGE
*   Student Activities and Study Guide, pp. 215-218
*   Transparencies 1, 41
*   Unit 6 Resource Book, pp. 9-12
*   Lesson 31-2 Spanish Resources

Focus
*   Write "What partnerships have you formed?" on the board. Discuss.

Teach
*   How Is a Partnership Created? (pp. 473-475)
*   Kinds of Partnerships and Partners (pp. 475-476)
*   Ending a Partnership (p. 477)
*   What's Your Verdict? (pp. 473, 475, 477)
*   Cultural Diversity in Law, *Commonwealth of Independent States* (p. 475)
*   FYI (p. 475)
*   Curriculum Connection, *Communication* (TE, p. 474)
*   Think Critically Through Visuals (TE, pp. 476, 477)

Apply
*   Think About Legal Concepts 1-6 (p. 478)
*   Think Critically About Evidence 7-12 (p. 478)

Assess
*   Lesson 31-2 Quiz (Unit 6 Resource Book, p. 9)
*   Reteach
Have pairs of students make a list of vocabulary words and their definitions. Then have students quiz each
    other on the definitions.
*   Enrich
    Invite someone from your community who is involved in a business partnership to speak to your class.
    Have students prepare a list of questions that include the following: What type of business is this?
    Why was the partnership formed? What type of partnership is it? What are the advantages and
    disadvantages of your partnership?

Close
*   Review questions in *What's Your Verdict?* on pages 473, 475, and 477.

Law for Business and Personal Use

Teacher: _____
Week of: _____
M   T   W   Th   F

Lesson 31-3   Operating Partnerships
Pages 479-483

Goals
- Discuss a partner's rights and duties
- Determine when a partner has authority to act
- Discuss a partner's potential liability

Teaching Resources
LAW LEARNING PACKAGE
- Student Activities and Study Guide, pp. 219-222
- Transparency 1
- Unit 6 Resource Book, pp. 13-16
- Lesson 31-3 Spanish Resources

Focus
- Write five duties of a partner on the board. Discuss.

Teach
- Partners' Duties (p. 479)
- Partners' Rights and Authority (pp. 479-481)
- Partners' Liabilities (p. 482)
- What's Your Verdict? (pp. 479, 482)
- In This Case (pp. 480, 481)
- Curriculum Connection, *Communication* (TE, p. 481)
- Think Critically Through Visuals (TE, pp. 480, 482)

Apply
- Think About Legal Concepts 1-5 (p. 483)
- Think Critically About Evidence 6-8 (p. 483)

Assess
- Lesson 31-3 Quiz (Unit 6 Resource Book, p. 13)
- Reteach
Have students use butcher paper to create a large mural that illustrates with drawings, pictures, and articles the characteristics of partnerships, including liabilities, duties, rights, authority, and kinds of partnerships.
- Enrich
Invite a local attorney who specializes in forming and dissolving partnerships to speak to the class. Have students prepare questions before the speaker arrives.

Close
- Have students write a lesson summary. Call on various students to read their summaries in class.

Law for Business and Personal Use

Chapter 31 in Review
Pages 484-487

Teaching Resources
LAW LEARNING PACKAGE
- Chapter 31 Test (Unit 6 Resource Book, pp. 17-18)
- Interactive Business Law Study Guide Chapter 31
- WESTEST Chapter 31

Review
- Concepts in Brief 1-9 (p. 484)
- Your Legal Vocabulary 1-12 (p. 484)
- Review Legal Concepts 13-16 (p. 485)
- Write About Legal Concepts 17-19 (p. 485)
- Think Critically About Evidence 20-23 (p. 485)
- Analyze Real Cases 24-29 (p. 486)

Apply
- Case for Legal Thinking (p. 487)
  - Practice Judging 1-2

Assess
- WESTEST Chapter 31
- Chapter 31 Test (Unit 6 Resource Book, pp. 17-18)

Law for Business and Personal Use

Teacher: _____

Week of: _____

M   T   W   Th   F

Chapter 32   **Creating, Running, and**
                 Terminating a Corporation
                 pp. 488-507

Introduction
- Hot Debate (p. 488)

Chapter 32 Teaching Resources
LAW LEARNING PACKAGE
- Unit 6 Resource Book, pp. 23-36
- Transparencies 1, 2, 42, 43, 44
- Student Activities and Study Guide, pp. 223-232
- Lessons 32-1, 32-2, and 32-3 Spanish Resources
- Interactive Business Law Study Guide Chapter 32
- WESTEST Chapter 32

Law for Business and Personal Use   Teacher: _____
                                                       Week of: _____
                                                           M   T   W   Th   F

Lesson 32-1   Creating a Corporation
Pages 489-493

Goals
- Describe what a corporation is and why it is the preferred form of organization for large business firms
- Identify different types of corporations
- Discuss how a corporation is formed

Teaching Resources
LAW LEARNING PACKAGE
- Student Activities and Study Guide, pp. 223-226
- Transparencies 1, 42
- Unit 6 Resource Book, pp. 23-26
- Lesson 32-1 Spanish Resources

Focus
- Discuss what students know about corporations, including foreign corporations.

Teach
- Advantages of Corporations (pp. 489-490)
- Disadvantages of Corporations (p. 490)
- Different Types of Corporations (pp. 490-491)
- How Is a Corporation Formed? (pp. 491-492)
- What's Your Verdict? (pp. 489, 490, 491)
- Cultural Diversity in Law, *International* (p. 491)
- In This Case (p. 490)
- Curriculum Connection, *Social Studies* (TE, p. 490)
- Curriculum Connection, *Communication* (TE, p. 492)

Apply
- Think About Legal Concepts 1-8 (p. 493)
- Think Critically About Evidence 9-14 (p. 493)

Assess
- Lesson 32-1 Quiz (Unit 6 Resource Book, p. 23)
- Reteach

- Enrich

Close
- Write the vocabulary terms for the lesson on the board. Call on students to define the terms.

Law for Business and Personal Use

Teacher: _____
Week of: _____
          M   T   W   Th   F

Lesson 32-2   Financing, Operating, and Terminating a Corporation
Pages 494-498

Goals
- Explain how a corporation is financed
- Discuss the duties of corporate directors and officers
- Discuss the procedure for terminating corporations

Teaching Resources
LAW LEARNING PACKAGE
- Student Activities and Study Guide, pp. 227-230
- Transparency 1
- Unit 6 Resource Book, pp. 27-30
- Lesson 32-2 Spanish Resources

Focus
- Provide students with annual reports of several major corporations. Have students use the reports to find three facts about each company.

Teach
- What Are Shares of Stock? (pp. 494-495)
- Who Controls the Business of the Corporation? (pp. 495-496)
- Powers and Duties of Corporate Officers (p. 496)
- How Do Corporations End? (p. 497)
- What's Your Verdict? (pp. 494, 495, 496, 497)
- Law and the Internet (p. 497)
- Curriculum Connection, *Social Studies* (TE, p. 497)
- Think Critically Through Visuals (TE, pp. 495, 496)

Apply
- Think About Legal Concepts 1-7 (p. 498)
- Think Critically About Evidence 8-12 (p. 498)

Assess
- Lesson 32-2 Quiz (Unit 6 Resource Book, p. 27)
- Reteach
Give each student $1,500 of imaginary money to invest in stocks. Each student must decide whether to purchase common or preferred stock or a combination. Have students then follow their stock for two weeks.
- Enrich
Have students work in groups to prepare a brochure for a real or fictional corporation that would make someone want to invest in the company's stock.

Close
- Have students write a short definition for each word in this lesson and use each word in a sentence.

Law for Business and Personal Use

Teacher: _____
Week of: _____

M   T   W   Th   F

Lesson 32-3   Corporate Powers and Shareholder Rights
Pages 499-507

Goals
- Describe the powers of a corporation
- Discuss the rights of a shareholder

Teaching Resources
LAW LEARNING PACKAGE
- Student Activities and Study Guide, pp. 231-232
- Transparencies 1, 2, 43, 44
- Unit 6 Resource Book, pp. 31-34
- Lesson 32-3 Spanish Resources

Focus
- Write "What are three powers of a corporation?" on the board. Discuss.

Teach
- Powers of the Corporation (pp. 499-500)
- Rights of Shareholders (pp. 500-502)
- What's Your Verdict? (pp. 499, 500)
- A Question of Ethics (p. 502)
- Curriculum Connection, *Social Studies* (TE, pp. 500, 501)
- Think Critically Through Visuals (TE, p. 502)

Apply
- Think About Legal Concepts 1-5 (p. 502)
- Think Critically About Evidence 6-8 (p. 503)

Assess
- Lesson 32-3 Quiz (Unit 6 Resource Book, p. 31)
- Reteach

Have students work with peer tutors to tell in their own words what they have learned in this lesson and
    what impact the information in this lesson has on their future lives.
- Enrich

    Have students research how Bill Gates built Microsoft into a major national corporation and personally
    became one of the richest persons to ever live.

Close
- Read and discuss *Prevent Legal Difficulties* on page 503.
- Have students work in pairs to summarize this lesson.

Law for Business and Personal Use

Chapter 32 in Review
Pages 504-507

Teaching Resources
LAW LEARNING PACKAGE
- Chapter 32 Test (Unit 6 Resource Book, pp. 35-36)
- Interactive Business Law Study Guide Chapter 32
- WESTEST Chapter 32

Review
- Concepts in Brief 1-5 (p. 504)
- Your Legal Vocabulary 1-11 (p. 504)
- Review Legal Concepts 12-15 (p. 505)
- Write About Legal Concepts 16-18 (p. 505)
- Think Critically About Evidence 19-21 (p. 505)
- Analyze Real Cases 22-27 (p. 506)

Apply
- Case for Legal Thinking (p. 507)
  - Practice Judging 1-3

Assess
- WESTEST Chapter 32
- Chapter 32 Test (Unit 6 Resource Book, pp. 35-36)

Law for Business and Personal Use

Teacher: _____

Week of: _____

M   T   W   Th   F

Chapter 33   Forms of Organization for Small Business
pp. 508-521

Introduction
- Hot Debate (p. 508)

Chapter 33 Teaching Resources

LAW LEARNING PACKAGE
- Unit 6 Resource Book, pp. 41-50
- Transparencies 1, 2, 45, 46, 47
- Student Activities and Study Guide, pp. 233-236
- Lessons 33-1 and 33-2 Spanish Resources
- Interactive Business Law Study Guide Chapter 33
- WESTEST Chapter 33

Law for Business and Personal Use   Teacher: _____

                                                                          Week of: _____

                                                                          M   T   W   Th   F

Lesson 33-1   Traditional Small Business Forms
Pages 509-513

Goals
- Discuss the advantages and disadvantages of the limited partnership and subchapter S corporation
- Identify the type of information required from members of a limited partnership
- Compare and contrast forming a limited partnership with forming a subchapter S corporation

Teaching Resources
LAW LEARNING PACKAGE
- Student Activities and Study Guide, pp. 233-234
- Transparencies 1, 2, 45, 46
- Unit 6 Resource Book, pp. 41-44
- Lesson 33-1 Spanish Resources

Focus
- Write "How does a limited partnership or S corporation benefit small business?" Discuss.

Teach
- Limited Partnership (pp. 509-510)
- Subchapter S Corporation (pp. 511-512)
- What's Your Verdict? (pp. 509, 511)
- A Question of Ethics (p. 511)
- Law in the Media (p. 512)
- Curriculum Connection, *Communication* (TE, p. 509, 511)
- Think Critically Through Visuals (TE, p. 510)

Apply
- Think About Legal Concepts 1-7 (p. 513)
- Think Critically About Evidence 8-14 (p. 513)

Assess
- Lesson 33-1 Quiz (Unit 6 Resource Book, p. 41)
- Reteach
Point out to students that many partnerships fall apart because the partners hadn't planned how they
  would deal with different issues that would come up in the course of doing business. Have groups of
  students work together on a list of issues that could come up when forming a partnership.
- Enrich
  Invite a local attorney to speak to the class about the ethics of law when working with clients who want
  to form a partnership or S corporation. Ask the attorney to answer questions such as: How is the fee
  decided? Is it ethical to charge large corporations more per hour than smaller corporations?

Close
- Have students work in pairs to write a summary of the information in this lesson. Have volunteers read
  their summaries to the class.

Law for Business and Personal Use

Teacher: _____

Week of: _____

M   T   W   Th   F

Lesson 33-2   New and Evolving Small Business Forms
Pages 514-517

Goals
- Explain how limited liability companies and partnerships are organized
- List the relative advantages of the LLC and LLP
- Identify the disadvantages in an LLC and LLP

Teaching Resources
LAW LEARNING PACKAGE
- Student Activities and Study Guide, pp. 235-236
- Transparencies 1, 47
- Unit 6 Resource Book, pp. 45-48
- Lesson 33-2 Spanish Resources

Focus
- Write "Why is the information in the lesson important to me?" Have students journal their answers. (See *Focus* section of TE on p. 514 for further explanations.)

Teach
- Limited Liability Corporations (LLC) (pp. 514-515)
- Limited Liability Partnership (p. 516)
- What's Your Verdict? (pp. 514, 516)
- Cultural Diversity in Law, *Wyoming* (p. 514)
- FYI (p. 516)
- Think Critically Through Visuals (TE, pp. 515, 516)

Apply
- Think About Legal Concepts 1-6 (p. 517)
- Think Critically About Evidence 7-11 (p. 517)

Assess
- Lesson 33-2 Quiz (Unit 6 Resource Book, p. 45)
- Reteach
Invite students to work together in pairs to write a poem or song lyrics that summarize this lesson.
- Enrich
  Have student groups create a company and a product. Then they are to create a brochure as a marketing tool to attract investors. The brochure must specify what type of corporation this is and the advantages of this type of corporation to the investors.

Close
- Read and discuss *Prevent Legal Difficulties* on page 517.
- Review this lesson by having students write an essay using every vocabulary word in a way that defines the word.

Law for Business and Personal Use

Chapter 33 in Review
Pages 518-521

Teaching Resources
LAW LEARNING PACKAGE
- Chapter 33 Test (Unit 6 Resource Book, pp. 49-50)
- Interactive Business Law Study Guide Chapter 33
- WESTEST Chapter 33

Review
- Concepts in Brief 1-9 (p. 518)
- Your Legal Vocabulary 1-6 (p. 518)
- Review Legal Concepts 7-10 (p. 519)
- Write About Legal Concepts 11-13 (p. 519)
- Think Critically About Evidence 14-17 (p. 519)
- Analyze Real Cases 18-23 (p. 520)

Apply
- Case for Legal Thinking (p. 521)
  - Practice Judging 1-3

Assess
- WESTEST Chapter 33
- Chapter 33 Test (Unit 6 Resource Book, pp. 49-50)

Law for Business and Personal Use

Teacher: _____

Week of: _____

| M | T | W | Th | F |

Chapter 34   Government Regulation of Business
pp. 522-533

Introduction
- Hot Debate (p. 522)

Chapter 34 Teaching Resources
LAW LEARNING PACKAGE
- Unit 6 Resource Book, pp. 53-62
- Transparencies 1, 2
- Student Activities and Study Guide, pp. 237-240
- Lessons 34-1 34-2 Spanish Resources
- Interactive Business Law Study Guide Chapter 34
- WESTEST Chapter 34

Law for Business and Personal Use   Teacher: _____
                                               Week of: _____
                                                 M   T   W   Th   F

Lesson 34-1   Constitutional and Historical Basis for Regulation
Pages 523-526

Goals
- Discuss the historical background that led to the formation of administrative agencies
- List the advantages of agency regulation
- Explain how a person can appeal decisions made by administrative agencies

Teaching Resources
LAW LEARNING PACKAGE
- Student Activities and Study Guide, pp. 237-238
- Transparencies 1, 2
- Unit 6 Resource Book, pp. 53-56
- Lesson 34-1 Spanish Resources

Focus
- Have groups of students create a new game. (See page 523 of the TE for details.)
- Ask what the two main decisions that had to be made when creating the game.
- Ask why it is important to have rules.

Teach
- Why Are Administrative Agencies Needed? (pp. 523-526)
- What's Your Verdict? (p. 526)
- Cultural Diversity in Law, *International* (p. 525, TE p. 524)
- A Question of Ethics (p. 526)
- Law and the Internet (p. 524)
- Think Critically Through Visuals (TE, p. 525)

Apply
- Think About Legal Concepts 1-5 (p. 526)
- Think Critically About Evidence 6-10 (p. 526)

Assess
- Lesson 34-1 Quiz (Unit 6 Resource Book, p. 53)
- Reteach
Invite a representative or an attorney from a local environmental organization to speak to the class about how the law can be used to help the environment.
- Enrich
  Have students work in groups to research careers in law or working for different government agencies. Break students into groups by interest. Have groups give oral reports to the whole class.

Close
- Review questions in *What's Your Verdict?* on page 523.

Law for Business and Personal Use   Teacher: _____
                                                       Week of: _____
                                                       M   T   W   Th   F

Lesson 34-2   Areas of Regulation
Pages 527-529

Goals
- Describe the areas of responsibility for the major agencies
- Discuss limitations on governmental regulation of business

Teaching Resources
LAW LEARNING PACKAGE
- Student Activities and Study Guide, pp. 239-240
- Transparency 1
- Unit 6 Resource Book, pp. 57-60
- Lesson 34-2 Spanish Resources

Focus
- Write "Should government have more or less control over business?" on the board. Discuss.

Teach
- Major Agencies and Their Areas of Regulation (pp. 527-528)
- Limitations on Agency Powers (p. 528)
- What's Your Verdict? (pp. 527, 528)
- Law in the Media (TE, p. 528)
- Think Critically Through Visuals (TE, p. 528)

Apply
- Think About Legal Concepts 1-6 (p. 529)
- Think Critically About Evidence 7-14 (p. 529)

Assess
- Lesson 34-2 Quiz (Unit 6 Resource Book, p. 57)
- Reteach
Have students record the events of a day in their lives and the agencies that have some connection to
    these events. To help students get started, brainstorm ideas, such as the hamburger they had for
    lunch was tested by the FDA, the hairdryer they used was regulated by the CPSC, and so on.
- Enrich
  Invite members of federal and state governmental agencies to speak to the class about their agency.
  Other options are for students to write to obtain literature or to have an agency day where students
  learn about the different agencies and careers available in them.

Close
- Read and discuss *Prevent Legal Difficulties* on page 529.
- Have each student read the text and write ten questions about this lesson. Then pair students and
  have them ask each other their questions.

Law for Business and Personal Use

Teacher: _____
Week of: _____
       M   T   W   Th   F

Chapter 34 in Review
Pages 530-533

Teaching Resources
LAW LEARNING PACKAGE
* Chapter 34 Test (Unit 6 Resource Book, pp. 61-62)
* Interactive Business Law Study Guide Chapter 34
* WESTEST Chapter 34

Review
* Concepts in Brief 1-7 (p. 530)
* Your Legal Vocabulary 1-11 (p. 530)
* Review Legal Concepts 12-16 (p. 531)
* Write About Legal Concepts 17-19 (p. 531)
* Think Critically About Evidence 20-24 (p. 531)
* Analyze Real Cases 25-30 (p. 532)

Apply
* Case for Legal Thinking (p. 533)
    * Practice Judging 1-3

Assess
* WESTEST Chapter 34
* Chapter 34 Test (Unit 6 Resource Book, pp. 61-62)

Unit 6 Forms of Business Organizations   (Chapters 31-34)
pp. 466-535
Wrap-Up
* Entrepreneurs and the Law (pp. 534-535)
    * Project 6 Forms of Business Organizations

Law for Business and Personal Use   Teacher: _____
                                                   Week of: _____
                                                        M   T   W   Th   F

Unit 7 Borrowing Money and Paying Bills   (Chapters 35-39)
pp. 536-611
Introduction
- In Practice Profile: Melissa Kugler, Bank Teller (p. 537)

Chapter 35   Commercial Paper
pp. 538-549
Introduction
- Hot Debate (p. 538)

Chapter 35 Teaching Resources
LAW LEARNING PACKAGE
- Unit 7 Resource Book, pp. 5-14
- Transparencies 1, 2, 49, 50, 51
- Student Activities and Study Guide, pp. 241-246
- Lessons 35-1 and 35-2 Spanish Resources
- Interactive Business Law Study Guide Chapter 35
- WESTEST Chapter 35

Law for Business and Personal Use

Teacher: _____

Week of: _____

M   T   W   Th   F

Lesson 35-1   Basic Types of Commercial Paper
Pages 539-542

Goals
- Explain the importance of commercial paper
- Describe the basic types of commercial paper and their uses

Teaching Resources
LAW LEARNING PACKAGE
- Student Activities and Study Guide, pp. 241-244
- Transparencies 1, 49, 50
- Unit 7 Resource Book, pp. 5-8
- Lesson 35-1 Spanish Resources

Focus
- Write "Upbeat Music Center" on the board
- Provide each student with a blank check. Have students make out the check to Upbeat Music Center to pay for compact discs that cost $45. Then discuss how a check is properly filled out.

Teach
- What Is Commercial Paper? (p. 539)
- Types of Commercial Paper (pp. 539-542)
- What's Your Verdict? (p. 539)
- In This Case (p. 540)
- Think Critically Through Visuals (TE, pp. 540, 541)

Apply
- Think About Legal Concepts 1-5 (p. 542)
- Think Critically About Evidence 6-8 (p. 542)

Assess
- Lesson 35-1 Quiz (Unit 7 Resource Book, p. 5)
- Reteach
Based on class discussions and reading, have students orally identify and describe the most important issues regarding commercial paper.
- Enrich
Have students write a paragraph discussing the meaning of the phrase, "Banks are debtors of their depositors."

Close
- Review questions in the two *What's Your Verdict?* features on page 539.

Law for Business and Personal Use

Teacher: _____

Week of: _____

    M   T   W   Th   F

Lesson 35-2   Specialized Forms of Commercial Paper
Pages 543-545

Goals
- Identify the various specialized forms
- Explain the purpose of the specialized forms
- Describe how and when to properly use them

Teaching Resources
LAW LEARNING PACKAGE
- Student Activities and Study Guide, pp. 245-246
- Transparencies 1, 2, 51
- Unit 7 Resource Book, pp. 9-12
- Lesson 35-2 Spanish Resources

Focus
- Tell students that in addition to the four types of frequently used commercial paper discussed in Lesson 35-1, five other forms are designed to meet specialized needs. These provide for safe, noncash means of transfer of monetary value.

Teach
- Specialized Forms of Commercial Paper (pp. 543-544)
- What's Your Verdict? (p. 543)
- Cultural Diversity in Law, *International* (p. 544)
- A Question of Ethics (p. 543)
- Think Critically Through Visuals (TE, p. 544)

Apply
- Think About Legal Concepts 1-5 (p. 545)
- Think Critically About Evidence 6-9 (p. 545)

Assess
- Lesson 35-2 Quiz (Unit 7 Resource Book, p. 9)
- Reteach
Have students create a fishbone map to visually illustrate the five key specialized forms of commercial paper.
- Enrich
Have students create posters to hang in a local bank or travel agency to advertise the benefits of traveler's checks. Have students include, at minimum, the advantages of traveler's checks, the process for acquiring and using them, and the advantages of this type of commercial paper over cash.

Close
- Read and discuss *Prevent Legal Difficulties* on page 545.
- Separate the class into five groups. Assign each group one of the five types of commercial paper discussed in this lesson. The groups may choose from any of the following: cartoons, poetry, rap, or posters. Create a bulletin board titled *Prevent Legal Difficulties When Using Commercial Paper.*

Law for Business and Personal Use

Chapter 35 in Review
Pages 546-549

Teaching Resources
LAW LEARNING PACKAGE
* Chapter 35 Test (Unit 7 Resource Book, pp. 13-14)
* Interactive Business Law Study Guide Chapter 35
* WESTEST Chapter 35

Review
* Concepts in Brief 1-5 (p. 546)
* Your Legal Vocabulary 1-12 (p. 546)
* Review Legal Concepts 13-17 (p. 547)
* Write About Legal Concepts 18-20 (p. 547)
* Think Critically About Evidence 21-24 (p. 547)
* Analyze Real Cases 25-30 (p. 548)

Apply
* Case for Legal Thinking (p. 549)
  * Practice Judging 1-3

Assess
* WESTEST Chapter 35
* Chapter 35 Test (Unit 7 Resource Book, pp. 13-14)

Law for Business and Personal Use   Teacher: _____
                                                   Week of: _____
                                                     M   T   W   Th   F

Chapter 36   Negotiability and Negotiation of Commercial Paper
pp. 550-563

Introduction
- Hot Debate (p. 550)

Chapter 36 Teaching Resources
LAW LEARNING PACKAGE
- Unit 7 Resource Book, pp. 19-28
- Transparencies 1, 2, 52
- Student Activities and Study Guide, pp. 247-252
- Lessons 36-1 and 36-2 Spanish Resources
- Interactive Business Law Study Guide Chapter 36
- WESTEST Chapter 36

Law for Business and Personal Use

Lesson 36-1   Requirements of Negotiability
Pages 551-554

Goals
- Explain the importance of proper negotiation
- List the requirements of negotiability
- Identify when an instrument is negotiable

Teaching Resources
LAW LEARNING PACKAGE
- Student Activities and Study Guide, pp. 247-250
- Transparencies 1, 52
- Unit 7 Resource Book, pp. 19-22
- Lesson 36-1 Spanish Resources

Focus
- List a variety of consumer products on the board (as many as you have students in the class). Include inexpensive personal items (pack of gum), moderately priced items (CD, jeans), and major purchases (car, condominium). As students enter the room, have them write an estimated price beside an item without a price.
- Discuss which items would be paid for with cash? How might the other items be paid for?

Teach
- What Is Negotiation and Why Is It Important? (p. 551)
- Requirements to Make an Instrument Negotiable (pp. 551-554)
- What's Your Verdict? (p. 551)
- Cultural Diversity in Law, *International* (p. 553)
- Curriculum Connection, *Communication* (TE, p. 552)

Apply
- Think About Legal Concepts 1-5 (p. 554)
- Think Critically About Evidence 6-9 (p. 554)

Assess
- Lesson 36-1 Quiz (Unit 7 Resource Book, p. 19)
- Reteach
Have students write both a conditional and an unconditional promise to repay a loan of $50 to a friend.
- Enrich
  Have students create checks to illustrate: *payable on demand, payable at a definite time, bearer, bearer paper,* and *order paper.* Have them exchange checks and identify each as *negotiable* or *non-negotiable.*

Close
- Review questions in the two *What's Your Verdict?* features on page 551.

Law for Business and Personal Use   Teacher: _____

                                                        Week of: _____
                                                        M   T   W   Th   F

Lesson 36-2   Proper Indorsement and Negotiation
                   Pages 555-559

Goals
- Explain the ramifications of improperly transferring commercial paper
- Identify the various types of indorsements
- Use the proper indorsement(s) to achieve a chosen purpose

Teaching Resources
LAW LEARNING PACKAGE
- Student Activities and Study Guide, pp. 251-252
- Transparencies 1, 2, 52
- Unit 7 Resource Book, pp. 23-26
- Lesson 36-2 Spanish Resources

Focus
- Have students respond orally to the following *True* or *False* statements:
  1. If the transfer of commercial paper does not qualify as a negotiation, it is legally considered to be assigned. (True)
  2. Negotiation has no ability to give the transferee rights greater than those available if the paper is merely assigned. (False)
  3. Bearer paper may be negotiated by delivery alone. (True)

Teach
- How Is Commercial Paper Transferred? (p. 555)
- Types of Indorsements (pp. 556-557)
- What Is an Accommodation Party? (p. 558)
- What's Your Verdict? (pp. 555, 556, 558)
- A Question of Ethics (p. 558)
- FYI (p. 557)
- Curriculum Connection, *Communication* (TE, p. 555)
- Curriculum Connection, *English Literature* (TE, p. 557)
- Think Critically Through Visuals (TE, p. 556)

Apply
- Think About Legal Concepts 1-5 (p. 559)
- Think Critically About Evidence 6-10 (p. 559)

Assess
- Lesson 36-2 Quiz (Unit 7 Resource Book, p. 23)
- Reteach
Have students create a graphic organizer to illustrate the four different types of indorsements described in this lesson.
- Enrich
Have students make a list of questions to ask if they were asked to be an accommodation party.

Close
- Separate the class into five groups. Assign each group on the five tips in *Prevent Legal Difficulties* on page 559.

Law for Business and Personal Use

Chapter 36 in Review
Pages 560-563

Teaching Resources
LAW LEARNING PACKAGE
- Chapter 36 Test (Unit 7 Resource Book, pp. 27-28)
- Interactive Business Law Study Guide Chapter 36
- WESTEST Chapter 36

Review
- Concepts in Brief 1-7 (p. 560)
- Your Legal Vocabulary 1-11 (p. 560)
- Review Legal Concepts 12-17 (p. 561)
- Write About Legal Concepts 18-20 (p. 561)
- Think Critically About Evidence 21-25 (p. 561)
- Analyze Real Cases 26-33 (p. 562)

Apply
- Case for Legal Thinking (p. 563)
  - Practice Judging 1-3

Assess
- WESTEST Chapter 36
- Chapter 36 Test (Unit 7 Resource Book, pp. 27-28)

Law for Business and Personal Use

Teacher: _____
Week of: _____
     M   T   W   Th   F

Chapter 37   Rights of Holders of
                     Commercial Paper
                     pp. 564-577

Introduction
- Hot Debate (p. 564)

Chapter 37 Teaching Resources
LAW LEARNING PACKAGE
- Unit 7 Resource Book, pp. 33-42
- Transparencies 1, 2
- Student Activities and Study Guide, pp. 253-258
- Lessons 37-1 and 37-2 Spanish Resources
- Interactive Business Law Study Guide Chapter 37
- WESTEST Chapter 37

Law for Business and Personal Use   Teacher: _____
                                                       Week of: _____
                                                                M   T   W   Th   F

Lesson 37-1   Collection and Discharge of
                   Commercial Paper
Pages 565-567

Goals
* Explain the importance of being a holder in due course
* Tell how to qualify as a holder in due course
* Discuss the ways commercial paper is discharged

Teaching Resources
LAW LEARNING PACKAGE
* Student Activities and Study Guide, pp. 253-254
* Transparencies 1, 2
* Unit 7 Resource Book, pp. 33-36
* Lesson 37-1 Spanish Resources

Focus
* Write "If someone alters a check you have written, you must still honor it" on the board.
* Poll students to see how many believe the above statement is true. Discuss.

Teach
* Holder in Due Course (pp. 565-566)
* How Is Commercial Paper Discharged? (pp. 566-567)
* What's Your Verdict? (pp. 565, 566)
* A Question of Ethics (p. 566)

Apply
* Think About Legal Concepts 1-3 (p. 567)
* Think Critically About Evidence 4-6 (p. 567)

Assess
* Lesson 37-1 Quiz (Unit 7 Resource Book, p. 33)
* Reteach
* Review questions in *What's Your Verdict?* on page 565.
* Enrich
  Give two index cards to pairs of students. Have the pairs make up two scenarios: one about a holder and one about an HDC or an HHDC. Have students exchange index cards and identify the status of the holder.

Close
* Have three volunteers stand with index cards labeled *holder, HDC,* and *HHDC*. Then have them role-play a scenario in which bearer paper transfers from the holder to the HDC, and finally to the HHDC. Have each person explain, as the bearer paper is transferred, why he or she is so labeled.

Law for Business and Personal Use

Teacher: _____

Week of: _____

M   T   W   Th   F

Lesson 37-2   Defenses to Collection of Commercial Paper and Electronic Fund Transfers
Pages 568-573

Goals

- Explain the importance of the difference between limited and universal defenses
- Identify the various types of limited and universal defenses to the collection of commercial paper
- Discuss the rights and duties involved in electronic fund transfers

Teaching Resources

LAW LEARNING PACKAGE

- Student Activities and Study Guide, pp. 255-258
- Transparency 1
- Unit 7 Resource Book, pp. 37-40
- Lesson 37-2 Spanish Resources

Focus

- Point out that, although a holder runs the risk of not being able to collect, most commercial paper is promptly paid.

Teach

- What Are the Limited Defenses to Collection? (pp. 568-569)
- What Are the Universal Defenses to Collection? (pp. 569-570)
- Rights and Duties Involved in Electronic Fund Transfers (pp. 571-572)
- What's Your Verdict? (pp. 568, 569, 571)
- Cultural Diversity in Law, *International* (p. 571)
- A Question of Ethics (TE, p. 569)
- Curriculum Connection, *Math* (TE, p. 572)
- Think Critically Through Visuals (TE, p. 570)

Apply

- Think About Legal Concepts 1-7 (p. 572)
- Think Critically About Evidence 8-11 (p. 573)

Assess

- Lesson 37-2 Quiz (Unit 7 Resource Book, p. 37)
- Reteach
  Working in pairs, have students create a collage showing various types of EFTs in use in your community. They may use pictures from magazines or newspapers, illustrations, and/or photographs they have taken.
- Enrich
  Have students create cartoon strips highlighting what one should do to limit a consumer's liability against unauthorized EFT transfers. Collect and photocopy the cartoons into an EFT booklet.

Close

- Read and discuss *Prevent Legal Difficulties* on page 573.
- Have students work in groups to create a newspaper, television, or radio item stressing one of the five ways for a consumer to protect himself or herself.

Law for Business and Personal Use

Chapter 37 in Review
Pages 574-577

Teaching Resources
LAW LEARNING PACKAGE
* Chapter 37 Test (Unit 7 Resource Book, pp. 41-42)
* Interactive Business Law Study Guide Chapter 37
* WESTEST Chapter 37

Review
* Concepts in Brief 1-8 (p. 574)
* Your Legal Vocabulary 1-7 (p. 574)
* Review Legal Concepts 8-10 (p. 575)
* Write About Legal Concepts 11-14 (p. 575)
* Think Critically About Evidence 15-19 (p. 575)
* Analyze Real Cases 19-24 (p. 576)

Apply
* Case for Legal Thinking (p. 577)
  * Practice Judging 1-3

Assess
* WESTEST Chapter 37
* Chapter 37 Test (Unit 7 Resource Book, pp. 41-42)

Law for Business and Personal Use

Teacher: _____
Week of: _____
           M   T   W   Th   F

Chapter 38   Secured and Unsecured
                     Credit Obligations
                     pp. 578-591

Introduction
- Hot Debate (p. 578)

Chapter 39 Teaching Resources
LAW LEARNING PACKAGE
- Unit 7 Resource Book, pp. 47-56
- Transparencies 1, 2, 54
- Student Activities and Study Guide, pp. 259-264
- Lessons 38-1 and 38-2 Spanish Resources
- Interactive Business Law Study Guide Chapter 38
- WESTEST Chapter 38

Law for Business and Personal Use

Teacher: _____

Week of: _____

M   T   W   Th   F

Lesson 38-1   Establishing a Security Interest
Pages 579-581

Goals
- Distinguish between debtors and creditors
- Discuss the importance of protecting both creditors and debtors
- Describe a secured transaction

Teaching Resources
LAW LEARNING PACKAGE
- Student Activities and Study Guide, pp. 269-270
- Transparencies 1, 2
- Unit 7 Resource Book, pp. 47-50
- Lesson 38-1 Spanish Resources

Focus
- Write "Who are debtors and credits?" on the board. Have students write examples of each before class begins.

Teach
- Who Are Debtors and Creditors? (p. 579)
- What Is a Secured Transaction? (pp. 580-581)
- What's Your Verdict? (pp. 579, 580)
- A Question of Ethics (p. 579)
- Law and the Internet (p. 580)
- FYI (p. 579)
- Cultural Diversity in Law, *Columbia* (p. 580)
- Think Critically Through Visuals (TE, p. 580)

Apply
- Think About Legal Concepts 1-5 (p. 581)
- Think Critically About Evidence 6-7 (p. 581)

Assess
- Lesson 38-1 Quiz (Unit 7 Resource Book, p. 47)
- Reteach
Write the vocabulary terms from this lesson on the board. Have students who need help with the concepts write a definition under each term.
- Enrich
Have students explain in writing why repossession of tangible collateral must be possible in order to have a secured transaction in tangible property.

Close
- Review questions in *What's Your Verdict?* on pages 579 and 580.

Law for Business and Personal Use   Teacher: _____

                                              Week of: _____
                                              M   T   W   Th   F

Lesson 38-2   Creation and Perfection of
                   Security Interests
                   Pages 582-587

Goals
- Explain how security interests are created and perfected
- Determine how and when security interests are terminated

Teaching Resources

LAW LEARNING PACKAGE
- Student Activities and Study Guide, pp. 261-264
- Transparencies 1, 54
- Unit 7 Resource Book, pp. 51-54
- Lesson 38-2 Spanish Resources

Focus
- Begin class by discussing how the UCC changed creditors' rights with regard to the personal property of debtors.

Teach
- How Are Security Interests Created? (pp. 582-583)
- How Does a Creditor Perfect a Security Interest? (pp. 583-586)
- How Are Secured Transactions Terminated? (p. 586)
- What's Your Verdict? (pp. 582, 583, 586)
- In This Case (p. 585)
- A Question of Ethics (TE, p. 586)
- Cultural Diversity in Law (TE, p. 583)
- Curriculum Connection, *Communication* (TE, pp. 582, 585)
- Curriculum Connection, *Art* (TE, p. 586)
- Think Critically Through Visuals (TE, p. 584)

Apply
- Think About Legal Concepts 1-4 (p. 587)
- Think Critically About Evidence 5-7 (p. 587)

Assess
- Lesson 38-2 Quiz (Unit 7 Resource Book, p. 51)
- Reteach

Have students create a graphic organizer with the words *Terminated Transaction* in the center circle. Then connect two smaller circles, *Paid in Full* and *Defaulted.* Have students provide information about what happens to debtors and creditors when a transaction is terminated in either manner.
- Enrich

Have students write three *True or False* statements about how secured transactions are terminated. Have volunteers read their statements and class members answer.

Close
- Read and discuss *Prevent Legal Difficulties* on page 587.

Law for Business and Personal Use

Teacher: _____

Week of: _____

M   T   W   Th   F

Chapter 38 in Review
Pages 588-591

Teaching Resources
LAW LEARNING PACKAGE
- Chapter 38 Test (Unit 7 Resource Book, pp. 55-56)
- Interactive Business Law Study Guide Chapter 38
- WESTEST Chapter 38

Review
- Concepts in Brief 1-7 (p. 588)
- Your Legal Vocabulary 1-8 (p. 588)
- Review Legal Concepts 9-12 (p. 589)
- Write About Legal Concepts 13-15 (p. 589)
- Think Critically About Evidence 16-19 (p. 589)
- Analyze Real Cases 20-26 (p. 590)

Apply
- Case for Legal Thinking (p. 591)
  - Practice Judging 1-2

Assess
- WESTEST Chapter 38
- Chapter 38 Test (Unit 7 Resource Book, pp. 55-56)

Law for Business and Personal Use   Teacher: _____
                                             Week of: _____
                                             M   T   W   Th   F

Chapter 39   Debtors, Creditors, and Bankruptcy
                       pp. 592-609

Introduction
- Hot Debate (p. 592)

Chapter 39 Teaching Resources
LAW LEARNING PACKAGE
- Unit 7 Resource Book, pp. 61-74
- Transparencies 1, 2, 54, 56
- Student Activities and Study Guide, pp. 265-275
- Lessons 39-1, 39-2, and 39-3 Spanish Resources
- Interactive Business Law Study Guide Chapter 39
- WESTEST Chapter 39

Law for Business and Personal Use

Teacher: _____
Week of: _____
M   T   W   Th   F

Lesson 39-1   Legal Protection of Creditors
Pages 593-595

Goals
* Discuss four types of laws that protect creditors
* Explain how liens are created
* Explain how liens can protect creditor's rights

Teaching Resources
LAW LEARNING PACKAGE
* Student Activities and Study Guide, pp. 265-268
* Transparency 1
* Unit 7 Resource Book, pp. 61-64
* Lesson 39-1 Spanish Resources

Focus
* Write "Why do people use credit cards?" on the board. Discuss and record student answers.

Teach
* Laws Protecting Creditors (pp. 593-595)
* What's Your Verdict? (p. 593)
* In This Case (p. 594)
* Think Critically Through Visuals (TE, p. 594)

Apply
* Think About Legal Concepts 1-5 (p. 595)
* Think Critically About Evidence 6-7 (p. 595)

Assess
* Lesson 39-1 Quiz (Unit 7 Resource Book, p. 61)
* Reteach
Working in small groups, have one student be the pawnbroker and the others be borrowers. Have
    students role-play pawning various (fictitious) items, bargaining over price, interest, and the time limit
    to buy back the items.
* Enrich
    Have students work in groups to create interview questions for pawnbrokers regarding their interest
    rates and other policies. Have each group telephone a pawnbroker and then present its findings to the
    class. Compare interest rates with rates from banks and credit cards.

Close
* Review questions in *What's Your Verdict?* on page 593.

Law for Business and Personal Use   Teacher: _____

Week of: _____

M   T   W   Th   F

Lesson 39-2   Legal Protection of Debtors and Use of Credit Cards
Pages 596-601

Goals
• Discuss six types of laws that protect debtors
• Discuss the advantages and disadvantages of using credit cards

Teaching Resources
LAW LEARNING PACKAGE
• Student Activities and Study Guide, pp. 269-270
• Transparencies 1, 2, 54
• Unit 7 Resource Book, pp. 65-68
• Lesson 39-2 Spanish Resources

Focus
• Write "Truth in Lending Act" on the board. Ask students how this act protects debtors. Discuss.

Teach
• Laws Protecting Debtors (pp. 596-599)
• Special Laws for Credit Cards (pp. 599-601)
• What's Your Verdict? (pp. 596, 599)
• A Question of Ethics (pp. 597, 599, 601)
• Law in the Media (p. 600)
• Law and the Internet (p. 598, TE p. 599)
• Curriculum Connection, *Social Studies* (TE, p. 596)
• Curriculum Connection, *Communication* (TE, p. 598)
• Think Critically Through Visuals (TE, p. 600)

Apply
• Think About Legal Concepts 1-5 (p. 601)
• Think Critically About Evidence 6-7 (p. 601)

Assess
• Lesson 39-2 Quiz (Unit 7 Resource Book, p. 65)
• Reteach
Have pairs of students make a poster informing their classmates what to do if a credit card is stolen or lost. Display the posters.
• Enrich
As a group, have students create a cartoon strip to illustrate the perils of misusing credit cards. You may wish to bring in sample comics from a daily newspaper for students to use as a guide to format.

Close
• Review by having students work in pairs. Each student is to write ten questions to ask his or her partner.

Law for Business and Personal Use   Teacher: _____

Week of: _____

M   T   W   Th   F

Lesson 39-3   Bankruptcy
Pages 602-605

Goals
- Explain the purpose and importance of the bankruptcy procedure
- Identify the various types of bankruptcy
- Discuss the limitations of bankruptcy in discharging debts

Teaching Resources
LAW LEARNING PACKAGE
- Student Activities and Study Guide, pp. 271-275
- Transparencies 1, 56
- Unit 7 Resource Book, pp. 69-72
- Lesson 39-3 Spanish Resources

Focus
- Write "What is bankruptcy?" on the board. Have students answer this question in writing as they enter the classroom.

Teach
- What Is Bankruptcy? (pp. 602-603)
- Procedure for Chapter 7 Bankruptcy (pp. 603-604)
- What's Your Verdict? (pp. 602, 603)
- Cultural Diversity in Law, *Great Britain* (p. 602)
- Curriculum Connection, *Communication* (TE, p. 603)
- Think Critically Through Visuals (TE, p. 604)

Apply
- Think About Legal Concepts 1-4 (p. 605)
- Think Critically About Evidence 5-8 (p. 605)

Assess
- Lesson 39-3 Quiz (Unit 7 Resource Book, p. 69)
- Reteach
Have students use the information on page 604 to create a two-column chart. In the first column, entitled *Debts Not Discharged*, have students list those debts not canceled by bankruptcy. In the second column, called *Assets Exempt from Seizure*, have students identify those assets exempt by federal law.
- Enrich
Have students explain why the claim of bankruptcy cannot discharge student loans. Ask students to hypothesize the intent of this exception.

Close
- Read and discuss *Prevent Legal Difficulties* on page 605.

Law for Business and Personal Use

Teacher: _____

Week of: _____

        M   T   W   Th   F

Chapter 39 in Review
Pages 606-609

Teaching Resources
LAW LEARNING PACKAGE
- Chapter 39 Test (Unit 7 Resource Book, pp. 73-74)
- Interactive Business Law Study Guide Chapter 39
- WESTEST Chapter 39

Review
- Concepts in Brief 1-6 (p. 606)
- Your Legal Vocabulary 1-10 (p. 606)
- Review Legal Concepts 11-16 (p. 607)
- Write About Legal Concepts 17-19 (p. 607)
- Think Critically About Evidence 20-24 (p. 607)
- Analyze Real Cases 25-30 (p. 608)

Apply
- Case for Legal Thinking (p. 609)
  - Practice Judging 1-2

Assess
- WESTEST Chapter 39
- Chapter 39 Test (Unit 7 Resource Book, pp. 73-74)

Unit 7 Borrowing Money and Paying Bills   (Chapters 35-39)
pp. 536-611
Wrap-Up
- Entrepreneurs and the Law (pp. 610-611)
  - Project 7 Borrowing Money and Paying Bills
  - Think Critically Through Visuals (p. 611)